What Readers

"Captivating, riveting, and in _____ tough to put down. Tanya's strength was tested on so many levels, and she has shown through her story that she is a survivor. Tanya has shown how anyone can survive depression and come out of it with a vibrant, healthy, and fulfilled life. Five stars for one of the best books I have read in a long time."

— Debra Rosen
President/CEO San Diego North Chamber of Commerce
Founder of San Diego Women's Week

"As someone who has suffered with depression for about forty years, I find it unbelievable that so many folks still attach a stigma and find it hard to accept the fact that it is a disease like diabetes or any other physical condition. One could say Tanya simply experienced many shattering emotional events that would bring anyone down, but that's not how depression works.

"As in my case, the groundwork was laid several years earlier in Tanya's childhood, waiting to rear its ugly head, and she suffered with the disease for many years before seeking the help that probably saved her life. This is an important book that talks about her suffering in terms everyone can relate to. Hooray for Tanya for her courage to expose the illness for what it is, and for her effort to encourage others to shed the fear of weakness and seek help earlier rather than later."

— Tony Dow
Actor, Director, Producer, and Sculptor

"Tanya takes readers on a healing journey with a straightforward and brave account of the chaos that was her life. Conflicted and isolated, she explodes with a cry for help that ultimately leads her to find truth within herself. A must read!"

— Eric Hipple
Former NFL quarterback
Author of _Real Men Do Cry_
Outreach Coordinator, Univ. of Michigan Depression Center

"Deep, powerful, and healing. These were the first words that came to mind when reading *Finding Peace Amid the Chaos*. But, I am not sure any words can do this book justice because the book is an experience that leaves the reader empowered with a sense of peace and a knowing that there are tools for anyone who has gone down the rabbit hole of depression or loss. Written from a true life authentic point of view, my spirit was moved and my soul evolved by reading such an amazing work."

— Ken D. Foster
Author, Speaker, and Business Intuitive

"Tanya Brown's story is gripping and compelling. The death of her sister, Nicole Brown Simpson, is an unimaginable loss, but Tanya's story is about far more than a murder and the loss of a sister. The depression she has overcome offers hope to all of us who have faced loss, suffered from darkness, or lost ourselves in circumstances beyond our control. Tanya's journey, written so honestly page after page, left me with a sense of victory and resiliency that we all long to find in life – no matter what our challenges and pain. This book is a testimony to the power of love, grace, redemption, and new dreams – no matter how dark the past, how great the pain, and no matter what others have done to us."

— Casey Gwinn, Esq.
President, National Family Justice Center Alliance

"*Finding Peace Amid the Chaos* provides the reader with heart-felt stories and solutions for dealing with major life challenges and daily challenges. When you apply the lessons and strategies woven throughout the chapters, you will experience more peace of mind and calmness when life throws a curve ball."

— Dr. John Spencer Ellis
Executive Producer, *The Compass*
Founder, Wexford University

"In her breathtaking book, *Finding Peace Amid the Chaos*, Tanya Brown shows us that it really is possible to move from a place of deep depression to ultimate triumph – while removing the stigma from mental illness. Tanya is one of the most down to earth people I have ever met and she keeps it real in her book as well, giving us her perspective on what it was like to go through a very public tragedy and her own personal challenges, while trying to find peace and truth. If you are going through a tough time in your life, or have at any time, you will be inspired and moved by her journey and words of wisdom."

— Ursula Mentjes
Two-Time Bestselling Author of *Selling with Intention, Selling with Synchronicity* and *One Great Goal*

"Tanya's story is highly personal, revealing her struggles with a series of relationship losses that culminated in a psychiatric hospitalization. In this memoir, Tanya courageously describes her struggles with depression, the loss of her voice for fear of her family being misjudged, living in the shadow of her larger-than-life older sisters, and how she finally gained the courage to face and express her authentic feelings and find support.

"Now a life coach, motivational speaker, and advocate for victims of mental illness, Tanya's story is a journey from post-traumatic stress to post-traumatic growth – from covering up her emotional struggles to actively confronting them and using her knowledge to inspire others, thereby honoring her sister's memory. The book culminates in a series of practical strategies and coping tools to soothe negative emotion and take constructive action in the face of emotional challenges. Tanya's story and tools provide understanding, hope, and help for survivors everywhere."

— Melanie Greenberg, Ph.D.
Clinical psychologist in Marin County, California,
National speaker, Trauma researcher,
Author of the bestselling Mindful Self-Express blog at
Psychologytoday.com; Consultant to national media

"Having battled chronic depression for almost thirty years, I know the very serious impact it can have on one's life. I urge those who have depression, and the families and friends of those who suffer from it, to read this compelling book. Each of our lives is as different as our individual fingerprints, but we can all learn from the lessons shared by Tanya Brown, whose courage and resolve are an inspiration."

— Tom Johnson
Former Publisher and CEO, *Los Angeles Times*
Former Chairman and CEO, Cable News Network(CNN)

"Tanya truly is a testament of courage to everyone. Her story will captivate your spirit and inspire you to live a happier life."

— James Malinchak
Featured on ABC's Hit TV Show *Secret Millionaire*
Founder of www.BigMoneySpeaker.com

"Tanya Brown's story is one of inner conflict, overcoming adversity, and finally of victory. It exposes, for all to see, the effects of depression as something real and debilitating, even life-threatening. For those who have suffered from depression, this is a means of gaining understanding and a guide to fighting back and regaining control. Bold, honest, realistic, relevant, and inspirational; Tanya has done an excellent job of bringing the disease, its consequences, and its treatment to life."

— Bil Howard
Readers' Favorite Book Reviews
5-star review

FINDING PEACE
AMID THE CHAOS

FINDING PEACE AMID the CHAOS

My Escape from Depression and Suicide

BY TANYA BROWN

Sister of Nicole Brown Simpson

WITH WILLIAM CROYLE

LANGMARC
PUBLISHING
Austin, Texas

FINDING PEACE AMID THE CHAOS

My Escape from Depression and Suicide

By Tanya Brown
with William Croyle

Cover layout: Michael Qualben
Cover photo: © David Le Bon

Published by LangMarc Publishing
P.O. Box 90488
Austin, TX 78709
www.langmarc.com

Library of Congress Control Number: 2013953657
ISBN: 1-880292-49-1 • 978-1-880292-49-5

For everyone suffering with mental illness, loss,
or struggles of any kind.
May you be blessed with the courage and grace
to find the peace and hope you deserve.

CONTENTS

FOREWORD

I sat next to Tanya during our group therapy sessions in South Coast Medical Center's psychiatric outpatient program. It was October 2004. As a fellow patient, I tried hard those first few days to get her to talk, but she wanted none of it. It was obvious she was very fragile, afraid of her own shadow, a frail girl trapped inside a brain on overdrive that was filled with pain, sorrow, and anger.

I initially had no idea who she was – the youngest sister of Nicole Brown Simpson, whose murder in 1994 became one of the most highly publicized cases in U.S. history. But once someone told me who she was, I was even more determined to find a way to make her feel at ease with the dozen other patients and group leader pressuring her to talk. I couldn't imagine the hell she'd been through.

Several times she was quick to anger, distrustful, and became a hermit within her own soul … scrunching in the chair, feet off the ground, and rocking with deep fright consuming her being. I tried to give her a pat on the back, or a hug. She would say in sharp voice, "Don't even think about it! Not a good time!" I'd step away and give her space.

Privately, with some careful persistence, I was finally able to get her to talk. I could see she was a great person, but she could not communicate. Though I was going through my own stuff, I gave her my shoulder, love, and comfort, everything that every one of us wanted but struggled to find and hold on to. She told me she had thoughts of ending it all. I told her that evil should not win, that together we could overcome our deepest and darkest fears and rise above them. Gradually, we formed a bond. We "got" each other. We found peace together. We built a trust with one another.

One day in our group session, the leader asked us again to share our stories, to tell why we were there, but Tanya was still not about to open her heart. So I opened mine. I finally told my story and, when I was finished, I turned to Tanya and said, "It's time." I held her hand as the floodgates opened. She told it all: from Nicole's murder, to having to endure the "Trial of the Century," to the deaths of her two closest friends, to her fiancé ending their engagement just days before their wedding. As difficult as it was for Tanya, I could see the life blowing back into her. From that point forward, she talked openly every day and started helping others as well. The Tanya I had gotten to know privately was blossoming, coming out with vengeance! She went from being a deeply depressed woman – a bundle of anger, nerves, and anxiety, hating everyone and thinking her life was over – to a flower that gracefully grew into full bloom to take on the world with energy, laughter, smiles, and a new-found confidence.

From that moment, Tanya became an advocate for every-one at South Coast, including me, and for people worldwide suffering with mental illness. I had been the one to reach out to her, never expecting that she would ultimately end up helping me, significantly impacting my health and future.

That bond we forged in 2004 will never be broken. Her gift of love and life will remain with me forever and will fill your heart, too, as you read her incredible story.

Kate Hughes
Mentor, Certified Mental Coach,
Speaker, and Former LPGA Player

Introduction

Like millions of Americans and hundreds of millions of people worldwide today, celebrated comedian David Letterman once quietly suffered with depression.

"This, I'm telling you – you get on an elevator and the bottom drops out," he candidly told Oprah Winfrey when she interviewed him on her television network in 2013. He did not immediately seek treatment for it, yet continued performing his popular late-night talk show.

"I just pushed through it," he said. "It's a sinkhole, and people who have gone through it know exactly what I'm talking about. It's a sinkhole."

He is absolutely correct. I know because I am one of those people.

I suffered through depression for almost fifteen years before being treated. I ignored the countless warning signs during what was a very oppressive time in my life, believing that I, too, could just push through it by living behind a mask of happiness. But the pressure became so crushing that I finally snapped on a Saturday afternoon in 2004, impulsively lashing out at my family and nearly taking my own life minutes later.

Talking about depression, or mental illness in general, was once unheard of and is still considered taboo by many people today. A broken leg? You need to do whatever is necessary to get that fixed and become healthy again. A broken mind? You need to get over it. That attitude likely contributes to these staggering statistics:

- One in four American adults and one in five youth ages thirteen to eighteen experience mental illness in a given year, according to the National Alliance on Mental Illness.
- An estimated 350 million people of all ages worldwide suffer with depression, the World Health Organization reports.
- Suicide.org states that untreated depression is the number one cause of suicide.

- There were 38,364 suicides in the U.S. in 2010, roughly one every fifteen minutes on average, according to the Centers for Disease Control and Prevention.

- Pentagon statistics show that among our brave and heroic military men and women, 349 took their own lives in 2012, an average of nearly one a day. That was more than the number of troops killed fighting in Afghanistan that same year.

Mr. Letterman's "sinkhole" reference about depression is on the mark. I've personally described it as feeling like my ankles are chained to massive immovable boulders. Every attempt to escape is physically and mentally exhausting, creating a thick, heavy, excruciating sensation of complete hopelessness.

There are different types of depression and the causes and symptoms can vary from person to person, but all of those who suffer with it have one thing in common: they feel isolated, as if they are the only ones in the world going through it. They are often afraid to admit it because of the stigma that still exists with mental illness. That was how I felt until I finally acknowledged I could no longer continue living the way I was living and sought and accepted help.

The day after my breakdown, I checked into the psychiatric unit of a local hospital. It was not a magic bullet – there isn't one for beating depression – but nearly three months of treatment there provided me with the tools I needed to manage my depression day by day, even minute by minute. The therapy was a long and tedious process, but one that saved me. It enabled me to reclaim my life and taught me how to live happily, productively, and successfully.

Now, for the first time since I was discharged in December 2004, I am publicly sharing the intricate details of my depression, how I busted those chains and clawed my way out of that sinkhole, and how I continue to beat it today. I am also – for the first time since my sister, Nicole Brown Simpson, and her friend, Ronald Goldman, were murdered outside Nicole's condominium on June 12, 1994 – sharing some interesting facts about what happened inside my family's home the day we found out Nicole was killed, and what I psychologically had to bear in the aftermath of her death.

For those looking for a salacious tell-all book about Nicole and her ex-husband, former pro football star O.J. Simpson, as some people outside of our family have written for personal gain, this is not it. While I do share some compelling and previously untold stories related to the murder, the purpose is to show how events can feed one's depression and to emphasize the importance of seeking help for that depression as soon as possible.

Two other primary pieces of my life that I provide in this book are some of my personal journal entries I wrote during my stay in the psych unit, along with information from my medical records. I want you to be able to see where I was psychologically throughout the healing process so that you can get a good grasp – and help erase some of that stigma – of mental illness. Some of the journals, records, and verbal outbursts I had may be a bit disturbing. Yes, I used some very inappropriate language at times (which I have disguised in this book with symbols), but that shouldn't come as a shock since we're talking about an illness of the human brain. Some of what I said or what happened to me may also come across as funny. Please don't feel like you shouldn't or can't laugh. Do it! I do, quite often in fact, as I look back at where I once was and at some of the things I said and did. For example, I still laugh out loud today at how I greeted the morning in my journal on December 18, 2004, which I share in Chapter 20. Mental illness is a very serious issue, but I have learned that laughter really is some of the best medicine.

I hope that sharing my journey helps guide you on your journey, that I assist you to help yourself as others have done for me. If you have "pushed through" depression to this point, you now need to take the next big step and shove it away for good. It is not easy. It will take a lot of hard work on your part. But no matter what difficulties are in front of you, no matter how alone you feel, no matter how dark life may seem even when the sun is brightly shining, you *can* do it! I have been where you are and can promise you that there is hope. I am living proof of it.

"They say the best revenge is success, and I'm ready to get revenge on depression! I have so much potential, and I know that my heart has the capacity to feed people love. It really does. I have been through so much that when someone comes to me with an issue, it's likely I have been there. I don't know what the future has in store for me, but wherever I go and whatever I do, I'm going to walk tall, dignified, and most importantly, real, because I am done being 'happy, happy, happy' in a fake way. I am going to grab hold of what I have in my life, live it, and live it large! AMEN!"

– Tanya's private journal entry on November 14, 2004, one month into her psychiatric treatment for major depressive disorder

Chapter 1

And the Oscar Goes To ...

Each of us has a mental breaking point.

It's that undignified moment caused by the overwhelming stress and aggravation of a volatile situation, when we finally wreak emotional havoc on those around us. For some of us, depending on our personalities and the circumstances we're facing, it may take just hours or days to surface. For others, it could take months or even years. But indubitably, the intense frustration that we have allowed to roil and swell inside our minds will eventually conquer our psyche and cause a spontaneous explosion, like lava shooting from a fiery volcano.

In other words, we blow a gasket, fly off the handle, wig out, go ballistic.

For me, it took almost a decade and a half before I erupted and less than two minutes to spew it all out. That infamous episode happened on a Saturday afternoon, October 9, 2004, in the normally warm and friendly confines of our Dana Point home on Southern California's Pacific coast. My entire family was there, and the damage I left behind was swift and widespread. Not one of them was spared my verbal assault.

"If it had been the Academy Awards, your performance would have won you the Oscar hands down," my sister, Dominique, one of the victims of my diatribe, later told me.

It was categorically a psychological breakdown for the ages, but it was certainly no act. In fact, at thirty-four years old, it was the first time in my adult years that I could remember finally having the courage to be me. While it was lamentable and embarrassing that I unleashed my rage upon my family the way I did, it had to happen for my mental well being. It was a breakdown that would lead to my breakthrough and ultimately save my life.

The chain of events began unfolding that day around lunchtime when I grudgingly dragged myself out of bed and, in zombie-like fashion, shuffled into the kitchen. I went straight to the stocked wine cupboard, popped the cork off a warm bottle of my favorite merlot, squeezed it against my chest like a teddy bear, and retreated with it to my bedroom. No glass was necessary. Within a few hours, by late afternoon, the amount of wine left in the bottle had dropped as low as my self-esteem. At least what I consumed served a practical purpose by washing down the Klonopin pill I'd taken.

"Do not drink alcohol while taking Klonopin," the letters on the warning label screamed. "This medication can increase the effects of alcohol."

Haha! No kidding. But the last thing a pill-popping lush on the verge of a mental collapse is concerned about is a governmental instruction guide on how to properly drink.

I'd been prescribed the pills a month earlier after having a panic attack, and I was told to take them on an as-needed basis. That was like handing a five year old a bag of gummy bears and telling her to eat them only when she's hungry. I made the reckless decision that I "needed" the pills, and the wine, every day to try to ebb my emotional trauma.

That initial panic attack happened the first week of September after my fiancé abruptly severed our engagement, turning my life as a bride-to-be from a fairy tale into a business deal gone bad.

In the weeks leading to September 11, 2004, which was supposed to be our wedding day, I was focused on making sure all the details of the ceremony and reception were as picture perfect as I thought our relationship was. My fiancé, meanwhile, was evidently focused on our future – or, to be more precise, the possibility of a lack of one. While I was concerned about everything from the flowers to my dress to the food, he was concentrating on where his money would go if our marriage disintegrated. He was so worried about his business and assets being protected in case we divorced, that he – the man I loved and with whom I'd shared my life day in and day out for nearly a year – gracelessly presented me with a prenuptial agreement just ten days before the wedding.

He'd talked several months earlier about possibly drawing up a prenup, but he hadn't said another word about it since, so I'd never given it another thought. Now, with less than two weeks until we were to exchange our vows, it moved to the forefront of our nuptials, overshadowing the joy and exhilaration to which every bride should be entitled. I had the document reviewed by two well-known and reputable local attorneys, who both warned me that it would leave me with literally nothing if we ever split. I then brought it home and showed it to my dad. He was livid, and he let my fiancé and me know it.

"If this is who you are," he said to my fiancé, "then you are a huge disappointment to this family."

Dad then turned to me. "And if you sign this, I will not walk you down the aisle. I raised a smarter girl than this."

That was all I needed to hear to pressure my fiancé to do something about it.

"Don't worry," he assured me. "We will get this worked out."

He moved on to his next grand idea, which was to turn it into an incentive-laced contract. "How about if we're married for this long, then you get this much, and if we're married for this long, then ..."

Oh my God! This was his idea of "worked out?" It sounded like a contract for an NFL running back. "If you play in this many games, then you get this much money. Gain this many yards and I'll give you this much more. But if you don't score this many touchdowns ... well ... sorry." This had to be a joke. Did I need to insert a no-trade clause in there? When could I become a free agent? Should I test the market and solicit offers from other men first? My marriage had become a negotiation, making everything so jaded.

"This is just so ugly!" I exclaimed to him. "Just ... no! No way! I'm not going to do this!"

"Okay, okay," he said, feeling my ire and trying to calm me down. "I'll take this back to my attorney and make sure it's fair."

Those were two words – "attorney" and "fair" – that I'd rarely associated with each other, especially after witnessing the circus act several attorneys performed at the criminal trial following the murder of my sister, Nicole, ten years earlier. That experience alone gave me plenty of reasons to feel uneasy about any attorney getting involved in any aspect of my life, especially my wedding day. But I could not fathom anyone – even a lawyer – doing anything foolish to jeopardize our marriage.

What should have made the entire dilemma easy to solve was that even though my fiancé's timing couldn't have been worse, I honestly wasn't totally against a prenuptial agreement. Don't get me wrong – of course I preferred not having one at all, but I understood that he was the one who built his business and that he was protective of it. One unique issue I had to worry about, though, was that I also worked for him. I was an official employee of his company. That meant if we ever divorced, I would also be out of a job, unless I wanted to work for my ex.

No thanks.

I needed to make sure that, if our marriage fell apart, a prenup didn't cast me into a cardboard box on Skid Row.

Fast-forward to four days before the wedding. It was early evening, and I was eagerly waiting for my fiancé at his home in Huntington Beach. He was getting the revised prenup from his lawyer. I expected it would be "fair," we would sign it, put it away, and never have to discuss the matter again. There was no way he was going to let money destroy the love we had for each other.

I was already in a romantic mood because I'd picked up my wedding dress on the way to his house. And though my cooking experience didn't go much beyond punching a few buttons to trigger the radiation of a microwave oven, I poured my heart and soul into preparing a nice home-cooked meal for us, even using the stove. The dinner was accented with goblets of red wine, soft music, and aromatic candles. Everything was perfect when he walked in the door. I greeted him with a big smile, warm kiss, and a "Hi, Honey!" He returned my greeting with a distraught, beet-red face and beads of sweat rolling off his forehead, as if his conscience had just battled a few rounds with his balance sheet – and was clobbered.

"I can't do this," he said hesitantly, his eyes wandering everywhere except into mine.

Wait a minute. What? I gradually retracted my smile.

"You can't do what?" I asked.

"I … I just can't do it," he repeated nervously.

I dropped my hands off his shoulders, took a step back, and looked at him with disbelief. *There is no way he is talking about our marriage,* I thought to myself. *No way! But what else could it be?*

"Say that again," I said in a tone daring him to do so. "You what?"

"I can't …"

"What do you mean you can't? You can't?" I totally freaked. My eyes bugged out and jaw dropped as I threw my quivering hands onto my head. "Did you just cancel our wedding? Did you really just cancel our wedding?"

He stared into oblivion, clearly answering my question by showing no reaction and saying nothing at all.

"You just canceled our wedding!" I ranted repeatedly in utter disbelief, pacing back and forth. "Oh my God! I can't believe it! It's in …" I paused to quickly do the math. I was so flabbergasted that I couldn't immediately remember what day it was. "It's in four days! Four days!" I continued. "And you can't … you can't do this? How is that even possible?"

He said nothing more. What could he say? He just trumped the year we had emotionally invested in each other with his commercial investments. I bolted into the bedroom, grabbed my suitcases, and slammed everything I owned into them (here's a tip: clothes don't make much noise when you "slam" them into a suitcase, so if you're ever in a situation similar to the one I was, make sure to rattle the clothes hangers, bang the dresser drawers, and keep yelling about whatever comes to mind to make sure your once-significant other in the next room knows your anger hasn't abated).

"Call me a cab!" I ordered him while I packed. That prompted him to peek his head into the bedroom and make a faint attempt to stop me, but my glare was enough to back him off and shut him up. I stormed into the living room, carrying a suitcase in each hand and my wedding dress under my arm, and I was gone without another word. When the cab arrived, I threw my luggage into it, climbed into the back seat, slammed the door shut (now there's something that slams with some bite), and sat dejectedly with my beautiful, but now useless, gown lying across my lap.

"Hang on!" I ordered the cab driver as he was about to pull away to take me home. I rolled down my window to give a shout out to the next-door neighbor, who was standing outside.

"Hey, guess what?" I screamed, dispensing one final jab at my fiancé. "He just canceled the wedding!" The neighbor stared at me like I was psychotic.

Nope, not yet, but I was getting awfully close.

"Yeah! Just like that, he ended it!" I shouted. "I'm not worth enough to him." The cab driver sat quietly and patiently before giving me a tense "Okay, are you finished?" glare in the rearview mirror. With the confused, speechless neighbor still staring at me, I finally rolled up the window.

"Get me the hell out of here," I said. "Please."

Of course, there are two sides to every story. My fiancé's recollection of how things transpired that day may be different, but this is how I remember them during what was an extraordinarily emotional time for me. I never in a million years anticipated my upcoming marriage would end that day.

I was so upset and in so much shock that I couldn't even cry. At least not right away. My blood boiled the entire ride home and into the evening when I went to bed. I was too angry to even tell my parents or sisters about it as I tried to first make sense of it all for myself. When I woke up the next morning after just a few rough hours of sleep, I was still fuming. How could he do this to me? To us? And over money? I didn't care about his stupid money. I cared about him. What was I supposed to do now? I didn't know where to turn or what to do next. Were we really not getting married?

That question was unequivocally answered that afternoon when I received a stunning phone call from the place where we were going to be married. It shouldn't have been "stunning" considering I knew my engagement was over after the way everything unraveled the day before – but it was.

"Ms. Brown?" a sweet but tentative young woman's voice said on the other end.

"Yes," I replied.

"Um … um …" She was obviously uncomfortable, and her next sentence explained why since it was a question perhaps she had never had to verbalize.

"Are you aware that your wedding was canceled today?"

That confirmation was when the dam broke and the tears flowed.

"Are you okay?" she asked sympathetically.

"Yeah, I'm fine," I said between sniffs, trying to stay composed. "Thank you for calling."

I hung up the phone and ran into my parents' bedroom to tell Mom what happened. I collapsed on the edge of her bed, bawling uncontrollably.

"He … He … canceled …"

"Tanya, calm down," Mom said, sitting down next to me and putting her arm around me. "What's going on?"

"He … canceled … He canceled our … I … I … can't … breathe." And that was no exaggeration. My lips started turning blue. My body became stiff. The word "breathe" was ironically the last word I was able to muster before I couldn't speak anymore, unable to explain to Mom that our marriage was over before it even started. I became completely incapacitated, falling into a state of unmitigated shock.

"Tanya!" my mom screamed in a panic, confused as to what was physically happening to me. "Tanya!" She placed her hands on my shoulders and shook me. Nothing.

"Tanya! Snap out of it! Breathe, Honey! Breathe! What were you trying to tell me? Tanya! Talk to me!"

It wasn't working.

"Tanya!"

Smack! Smack! Smack!

She slapped me on the cheeks with both hands, each strike a little harder than the previous.

"C'mon, Tanya! Tanya!"

"What? Mom? What …" I finally emerged from my trance and began breathing again. Mom released a deep sigh of relief and hugged me close to help me calm down and regain some control – enough for my lips and face to return to their normal shades and enough for me to talk through my sobs and explain to her what had happened. It felt like she held me for hours. I cried for what seemed like the rest of the afternoon.

The next day was when I got the doctor-prescribed Klono-pin and also started on heavy doses of the self-prescribed wine. From that point forward, my life spiraled out of control at a ridiculously rapid rate. I commenced full self-destruction mode by frequently downing pills and alcohol and struggling daily to find anything worth living for. It lasted for about a month – until that award-winning performance on October 9 in front of my family.

Chapter 2

... Tanya Brown!

The sun was brilliant with temperatures circling seventy degrees on a magnificent fall day. We'd opened all the doors and windows of our home, allowing the gentle breeze from the ocean a couple of blocks away to filter into every room. It really was as nice as it sounds, the kind of weather that virtually mandated everybody be in a good mood.

I was sitting in the living room with my dad, mom, and sisters, Denise and Dominique. Denise's friend, Irwin, a man she knew from her days as a New York City fashion model in the 1970s and 1980s, was also there. He was in town for work and stopped by to visit. Irwin is a numerologist, someone who studies numbers and their possible influences on our lives. During his visit, he went through numbers relevant to each of our lives, such as our birthdays and other personal dates, to try to predict what kind of year we could expect to have. It was something fun to do. Well, fun for everybody else. I was in no mood to participate in anything pleasant.

In fact, given the condition I was in, I had no business being anywhere within sight of another living creature. The label on that pill bottle was dead on. If the alcohol that made me irritable and irrational was the firecracker, mixing it with Klonopin was like lighting the fuse.

The conversation among those in the room who weren't chemically dependent at that moment, which was everyone but me, was perfectly innocent. It was light, entertaining, relaxed. Irwin's predictions had people laughing, marveling, maybe even dreaming. But I was in another stratosphere, heavily plagued with tension, anger, and anxiety. I was fidgety and aggravated by everything anyone said. My head pounded like a drum at a rock concert. Make that a heavy metal rock concert. A migraine had nothing on this. The voices in the room were like the high-pitched screeching from microphone feedback. I wanted to plug my ears every time somebody so much as chuckled. And when more than one person laughed or talked at once, I ... well, honestly ... I just wanted to punch them. Every sound made me cringe. I hated that they were happy. Hated that they were feeling good and enjoying each other's company. Hated their smiles. Hated their clothes. Hated our house. Hated our couch. Seriously? Our couch? Yeah, I truly hated everything about everything and everyone.

God! They all just need to shut up! I was furious, screaming inside my pulsating head. *Blah, blah, blah! Who cares what you're saying? Get a life! Don't you all have better things to do than sit around and talk about numbers all day? Here are some numbers for you: by the time I count to five, you will all shut ... the hell ... up!! One! Two!*

I was so irate that I couldn't even make it to five. It wouldn't have mattered. They were just going to keep on babbling, and the more they did, the more infuriated I got. Each of their words became more pronounced. Every sound they emitted came out slower and slower, scraping in the most annoying and maddening way across every bit of brain matter I had. I couldn't escape it. I felt like I was in the midst of a nightmare, endless voices swirling inside and around my head, heckling me, refusing to leave me alone, trying to drive me insane.

Shut up already! All of you! Stop it! Now! Just ... shut ... up ... now!!!

Irwin turned his focus to me as he talked about the significant numbers in my life. He related them to past relationships with guys I dated, and he was in the midst of tying them to my present relationships, which of course included my ex-fiancé, striking a serious chord. That was the final straw. The internal pressure became too forceful to contain. I couldn't take it anymore. I knew where I was. I knew who I was with. I knew we had a guest. I knew I was the only one feeling the way I felt. But none of that mattered. I could no longer suppress my rage. I was like that volcano – stirring and rumbling, splashing lava through the rim, threatening to explode. I held back as long as I could until, finally, I just said, "The hell with it," and shot it all out right from the gut.

Who knows if Irwin had anything good to say about my future. I never gave him the chance as I sprung from the couch and cut him off.

"It's all your fault!" I cried. But for some inexplicable reason, I was staring directly at my dad. The room fell completely silent. All eyes were fastened on me. Dad turned and looked at Mom, then back at me. He was dumbfounded, to say the least.

"What? Tanya, what's wrong?" he said.

"It's all your fault!" I screamed again, sticking my finger in his face for emphasis. I had no idea what that even meant. What was his fault? The numbers Irwin was rattling off? My failed engagement? That I hated the couch? Daddy had been a huge supporter of everything in my life. Whether I was right or wrong about something, he was always there to help me, to defend me. My accusation toward him made zero sense; he was simply a victim of being seated closest to me when I decided to impetuously blow. But, unfortunately for him and everyone else in the room, there was no stopping me. I was now the scalding lava cascading down the sides of the volcano, sharply slicing through everything in my path. I continued my tirade toward Daddy, still blaming him without specifying what I was blaming him for. Then I made my rounds like a raging lunatic.

"And you!" I yelled at my mom. Really? I was going to do this to Mom? She ranked as high, and probably even a notch higher, than my dad when it came to her support for me throughout my life. Her face was plastered with a look of incredulity as I roared at her and shifted all of the blame – for what, I still did not know – onto her. She watched me in stunned silence, and she really had no choice since I didn't shut up long enough for her to get a word in edgewise.

I moved on to Dominique. Now everything was her fault. She sat there stone cold, taking the high road by showing no reaction during my attack. She refused to be sucked into a verbal war and seemed content to just let me go on and make a fool of myself. Her restraint almost made it seem like she had been waiting for me to eventually let loose like this.

I pretty much spared Irwin my wrath. Even though something he might have said in his numerology may have triggered my explosion, I probably figured I should take it easy on him since he was our guest. Sweet of me, huh? The poor guy had to be wondering what he walked into that afternoon and where the nearest emergency exit was. I bet he never saw this in my future. Or, who knows, maybe he did. The number 666 had to be popping up on his radar as he watched my conniption. If nothing else, at least I gave him a fascinating story to take back to New York.

I wish I could specifically remember what I said when I screamed at Dad, Mom, and Dominique, but it was all a blur at the time and is still a blur – to me and to them. That's likely because they were so taken aback by my outburst and because I'm sure a lot of what I said was incoherent drivel. It's probably better that I don't remember.

And let's not forget Denise, who doesn't put up with any garbage from anyone and shows little mercy toward those who try to dish it out – even toward someone in my psychotic state.

Denise, twelve years my elder and the oldest of my sisters, had been designated by my parents as our family spokesperson for the media after Nicole's murder in 1994. It truly didn't bother me that she was assigned that role. But what did bother me was that I wasn't allowed to talk at all. The family's intentions were good – they thought they were protecting me, sparing me the pressure from the media. I was the youngest, the baby in the family, who they believed had no reason to speak as long as Denise could handle it.

The reality, though, was that they were asking me to keep everything locked up inside, the opposite of the person I felt I was. I always felt like I was the psychologist in the family, the one most willing to listen to people and give sound advice.

That was not only my nature, but it was my passion and major in college. Telling me to not speak was like telling me to not breathe.

How many people who followed the trial and everything our family went through even remember that there was a youngest sister named Tanya? Very few. It's not that it was about me – far from it. I didn't need people to know who I was. It's just that I was never given the opportunity to publicly express my feelings about my sister's death like I felt I needed to do for my own well being. I felt forced to keep it bottled up. I felt suffocated. And, right or wrong, I felt like Denise was the one holding the pillow over my face. Words cannot express how much I resented her for that.

Well, maybe a few invidious words of the four- or five-letter variety could.

"You're nothing but a selfish &*#%$!" I screamed at her.

Holy crap! Did I really say that, and to Denise of all people? I also threw in a few choice insults about her son, Sean. Wow, was I demented! If anyone needed proof I had gone over the edge, there it was. I was completely out of control and absolutely went off on her. But Denise, one of the strongest women I've ever known and one who has never backed down from a fight, was not fazed. While my abhorrent words and behavior may have pierced the others in the room, anything I threw at Denise bounced right off her. Come to think of it, that toughness is what made her such a great spokesperson to handle the ruthless media for our family during the trial. If I were going to assail one particular person in the room more than anyone else, she was not a smart choice. As I should have expected, she didn't shy away, and she fired right back at me.

"Get control of yourself!" she yelled. Yeah, right. Way too late for that. In fact, that comment from her made me even angrier and more frustrated. She was supposed to accept whatever I said, no matter how ludicrous … and keep her mouth shut like everybody else. How dare she have the nerve to yell at me when I was the one having the breakdown! This was my time to be mad. Tanya time!

"Don't tell me what to do!" I snapped back at her, bringing the argument down to an adolescent level. "I'm done being told what to do." The rest of the family watched silently as our verbal war spilled into the dining room, where Denise and I met nose to nose.

"You need coping skills," Denise shouted.

"I don't have any!" I yelled back.

"Well you'd better find some!" she quickly snapped.

"Arrrrrgh!" I banged my fists on the table, ran into my bedroom, and slammed the door behind me. This wasn't anxiety. It was rage. Total, 100-percent rage. I was consumed with more hatred than ever before, and it was aimed toward everyone who loved me the most. Ugh! I cannot emphasize how horribly ugly the situation was. It was really, really bad ... and I was just getting started.

"Get me the &*#% out of this house!" I screamed from behind my closed door, tossing in a few more obscenities to articulate my anger. "Just get me away from this &*#%*$@ family!"

I was standing at the end of my bed, not sure where to go or what to do next, when I spotted my pills on the nightstand. Though I'd already taken one for the day a few hours earlier, I let my rage instead of my brain dictate my fate and headed straight for the pills. At the foot of my bed was a long, narrow table with some candles and a precious Tiffany lamp that used to belong to Nicole. The lamp had a thick, heavy, metal base and a beautifully-designed glass shade on the top. As I started toward the nightstand, I stumbled into the lamp, knocking it off the table. I made a half-hearted attempt to grab it before it hit the floor.

Crash!

Oh God ... what did I just do?

A big chunk of the glass shade broke, leaving a huge, irreparable hole.

OhGodohGodohGod! I anxiously said to myself over and over as I fell to my knees to pick up the broken piece. That lamp had always meant so much to me, and I had always been so careful to treat anything that once belonged to Nicole with the utmost reverence. But ...

I stared at the hole in the lamp and at the now-meaningless piece of glass in my hand. I continued to feel regret, but just for a few more seconds. Then it was like I flipped a switch and didn't care anymore. I tossed the broken glass aside, stepped over the lamp, and indignantly continued toward the pills. I know I should have felt horrible for a very long time about what I did, but I was still so charged up about what just transpired in the living room that even my destruction of a cherished sentimental object wasn't enough to cool me down.

I snatched the bottle of pills from the nightstand, yanked off the cap, and poured the pills into my hand. Ten, fifteen, I don't know. All I know for sure is that it was a lot, ten or fifteen more than I should have had. I sat down on the edge of my mattress and ogled them. It was the first time all afternoon that I was actually calm and focused on something.

Then came that moment, the most foreboding moment I'd ever experienced.

This is it! I said to myself in my convoluted mind. *I'm done! I hate everybody! I hate my life! I hate it all!*

As I eyed the pills, the significant losses in my life that brought me to that rock-bottom pit clicked on, playing slowly and nostalgically in my mind like an old, crackling silent film. I could see Nicole's beautiful shining face smiling at me, but that was immediately wiped out by the blood at the crime scene, the funeral, the tabloids, the helicopters hovering over our home.

Five years prior to her horrific death, my best friend, Herissa, was killed by a hit-and-run driver after a festival, just down the road from my neighborhood.

In 2000 – six years after Nicole's murder – my best friend, Troy, who was like a brother to me, died in a cliff-diving accident. I envisioned the sheer joy I imagined he felt as he leapt off his favorite cliff, soaking in the breathtaking beauty along his descent, his family and friends blissfully watching from below ... but it would be for the last time.

Three very different people in the forefront of my life, each one whom I loved, adored, and admired with all of my heart and soul, were taken from me within an eleven-year period.

They all died young, without warning, in tragic ways. I never got to say a final good-bye to any of them. Their deaths would trigger a host of problems in my life, which I would later figure out were pieces of the more encompassing issue: my unacknowledged depression.

I just couldn't deal with the pain of it all anymore.

What is the point of living? Why go on? I asked myself. *Look at all the good they were doing in their lives, and it was all unfairly ripped away.*

My body trembled as I became more aware of where I was and what I was actually considering doing. I glanced over at the nightstand and noticed there was just enough wine left in the bottle – the one I'd started swigging earlier that afternoon – to force the pills down. I looked at the pills again, the fire inside me still burning strong.

Just do it! a voice in my head confidently encouraged me. Another voice, one of reason, was urging me not to. It was like the devil on one shoulder and angel on the other. The devil, though, firmly had my attention.

Just be done with it! End the pain!

I reached for the wine, wishing I had more, but happy to have any left at all. I swirled it around a few times, trying to collect every drop that was clinging to the sides of the bottle.

That's it! the voice said, getting louder with each word and pushing me to quit wasting time. *Pop the pills in your mouth and let the wine take care of the rest. Everything will be fine.*

In the same manner that I blew up in the living room, I knew I was about to do it again, but this time to myself. I was becoming more and more upset as the voice continued buzzing in my head, and I was ready to succumb to the temptation of ending it all. I had everything I needed. Now I just had to do it.

It's time! the voice said.

But would it all be enough? Did I need more pills? Should I go into the kitchen and get more wine? Would it make all the pain go away? It felt like the angel on my shoulder was making a last-ditch effort to put doubts in my mind about what I was about to do, trying to give me excuses not to do it, to distract me in any way possible. But it was too late.

Let's end this thing! the persuasive voice said. *What are you waiting for? Do it! Do it!*

Oh God. This was it. I promptly shut down my brain, raised the hand full of pills, closed my eyes, opened my mouth, and…

"Tanya!"

I jumped probably a foot into the air as Dominique snapped me out of my trance with a quick, harsh call of my name after flinging the bedroom door open. I glared at her, looked down at the pills and wine, saw the broken lamp on the floor, and realized where I was and what almost just happened. I was so befuddled as to how I'd gotten to that point, but I quickly recalled my living room rant just moments earlier. Backed into a corner and unsure of what to do or say next, I latched on again to my anger, which was about all I had left at that point.

"Somebody better get me the hell out of here before I hurt someone!" I shouted at Dominique, my voice elevating with each word as I started to get revved up all over again.

"I know," she said, still just as calm as when I'd chewed her out earlier. "Let's go. I'm taking you to Deana's parents' house."

I took a moment to process what she said before determining that was a good thing for two simple reasons: I liked Deana's family, and I did not like mine. I didn't know what Dominique's long-term plans were for me, or if she had any at all, but as long as she got me out of that house, I was all for it. I voluntarily set the wine and pills down and took a deep breath.

"Good," Dominique said, happy that I was finally listening to someone and being rational about something. She noticed the lamp on the floor and picked it up, setting it back on the table. She saw the hole in the glass and probably wanted to berate me to no end, but she continued to keep her composure. She turned and headed out of the room.

"Come on out when you're ready," she said.

CHAPTER 3

Blue Pajamas and Laceless Shoes

Though I agreed to follow Dominique's lead, I was far from convinced that I wouldn't eventually return to my room to finish off both bottles. But one thing was certain: it was not going to be on that day and probably not for at least several days. Once I escaped from that house, there was no way I was returning any time soon.

I kept it simple, gathering nothing but my four primary comfort items – pillow, stuffed bear, blanket, and blue pajamas. I then calmly – yes, calmly, for once – opened my bedroom door and walked out. From my bedroom to the front door was probably fifteen or twenty steps, and they'd be the longest fifteen or twenty steps I'd ever have to take.

With my head down and my eyes staring at the floor, I walked out of my room and right past Denise without saying a word. I'll admit it was tempting to look up and try to stare her down, maybe even brush my shoulder against her. Haha! How immature would that have been? Can you imagine the all-out brawl that would have likely ensued if I had so much as nicked her? But I thought better of it, thank goodness. At least I had a shred of sense left.

I continued silently, pushing my way through the thick tension in the living room where my parents and Irwin were still sitting. They remained tongue-tied. I slipped out the sliding glass door and into our courtyard, but I still wasn't in the clear. There was a door beyond the courtyard I had to go through to get to the driveway. I stood patiently in the courtyard for what seemed like minutes, though it was probably just a few seconds, before I started yelling again.

"If someone is going to get me out of here, they'd better do it now!" I shouted to Dominique, referring to her as "someone" to try to show how angry I still was at all of them. "Or else I'll just drive myself!"

Dominique came out immediately and led me into her white pickup truck. Neither one of us spoke on the short drive to Deana's parents' house, giving me a chance to calm down a little bit before we got there. Deana, one of my closest friends growing up, wasn't living at home anymore, but her parents were like my second parents. I had known them since I was in fifth grade. They knew me as well as just about anybody, and they knew the dynamics of my family and all we had been through with Nicole's death.

"Come on in, Honey," they said when we got there, already apprised of my situation by Dominique. As expected, they welcomed me with open arms, gave me a bed to sleep in, and offered me anything I needed. It was a safe haven for me, and Dominique knew that. She had little concern about me trying to hurt myself as long as I was in their house. She helped me get settled in before heading out.

"I'll talk to you tomorrow, okay?" she said.

"Okay, Mini," I replied, feeling a slight sense of relief. "Mini" was the nickname we affectionately gave Dominique. The fact that I called her that and not something less flattering showed how much I had calmed down and that I had screwed my head on a little tighter since we left the house. Of course, a "thank you for saving my life by barging into my room at just the right moment and for getting me out of that house" was what I should have said. But I still wasn't in the right frame of mind, or even certain yet that being alive was the best thing for me. And after snapping as harshly as I had at home, it was probably best that I kept my mouth shut as much as possible. I had no margin for error at that point. Beyond Deana's house, I had nowhere else to go.

I spent the rest of that late afternoon and evening in solitude, with Deana's parents checking on me every now and then – not forcing me into anything but just reminding me that they were there if I needed them. For the most part, I just lay in bed, stared at the ceiling, and contemplated everything that had happened that day. I tried to analyze why I snapped, why I did it when I did it, and what I was supposed to do from there. It was difficult to believe I had behaved as I did, and I was sorry for the things I said to my family. But as remorseful as I felt, I thought something good might come from it. I didn't know what and I didn't know when, but there had to be something positive. I mean, I was about to take my own life – things could only get better, right?

As evening set in, with my mind exhausted but my nerves still churning from my tirade at home, I went into the back room of their house and called my ex-fiancé, whom I hadn't talked to much since our breakup a month earlier. I know, maybe not the smartest move. Call it foolishness. Call it vulnerability. But it seemed to make sense at the time. I thought that if he was a big part of the problem, then maybe he could be a big part of the solution.

"I just need to get away," I told him several times during what was a nearly two-hour emotional and amicable conversation. "Let's go hiking in the mountains, somewhere where we can just breathe. Let's try to work this out."

The way I narrow-mindedly saw it at the time was that my problems started a month earlier when he and I split up. It seemed logical, or as logically as I could think then, to try to fix things between us. That, I thought, would make everything better – like jumping into a time machine and turning back the calendar a month. But as I would later determine, my problems went far, far deeper than my relationship with him, and actually began several years earlier. Any plans to go hiking were going to have to wait.

Mini called me early the next morning. I was in a much more tranquil state.

"How are you today?" she asked.

"Better," I said, trying to muster up a little bit of enthusiasm.

"So are you ready?"

"Yep. I'm ready," I said. I had no idea what she was talking about, but so far she hadn't led me astray. "What are we doing?"

"I got it all arranged. South Coast has a bed for you," she said. "Take a shower, put your pajamas on, and I'll pick you up in a half hour. You don't need to bring anything else."

South Coast Medical Center, right down the road from my house, is known today as Mission Hospital Laguna Beach. The beautiful, white, circular building overlooking the Pacific Ocean has a behavioral health department – a psychiatric unit for people to get treatment for mental disorders. During my youth, I probably would have referred to it by a slang term such as the "loony bin," "nut house," or "funny farm." And because of that stigma, many people in my position likely would have resisted entering such a place. But I didn't even consider fighting it. I didn't have the strength, nor could I think of any other options. Deana's parents loved me, but I'm pretty sure they weren't looking to permanently adopt a thirty-four-year-old with mental problems.

"Sounds good to me," I told Mini. "I'll be ready when you get here."

When she arrived at the house, I gave Deana's parents big hugs, climbed into Mini's truck, and set off on my new adventure. No, I didn't view this as an adventure in the traditional sense of the word. I wasn't thinking of it as something exciting or invigorating. But it was something different, which is what I needed. A change of pace. A chance for a new beginning. A chance to maybe find myself.

Mini took me straight to the emergency room where they led me into an empty glass room, a holding area where they could keep an eye on me and be certain that I would remain safe until they were ready to register me. During registration, they asked Mini and me questions about my outburst at home the day before, took away my shoelaces, and checked to make sure I had no sharp objects on me that I could potentially use to harm myself or others. That's when the magnitude of my situation hit me.

Wow, I thought to myself. *I always knew this place was here, but I never thought I'd actually be here one day. No shoelaces? This is serious stuff.*

But as serious as it was, it was also painless. I answered all of their questions honestly and had no problem conforming to everything they asked of me. Then, just as we were finishing up, Amy walked by.

Wait a second. Amy?

"Tanya?" she said, just as surprised to see me as I was to see her. Amy was an old neighbor and a good friend of mine. I never expected to see anybody I knew in a psych unit.

"What are you doing here?" I asked.

"I just started working in the ER," she said. "Soooo ... what are you doing here?"

I figured my new blue-pajamas-and-laceless-shoes wardrobe pretty much answered that question, so there was no sense in trying to hide anything from her. "I'm going crazy," I replied matter-of-factly, with a big smile on my face.

"Huh. Really?" she said.

"Yep. They said they've got a bed waiting for me."

She shrugged her shoulders. "That's okay," she said without judgment, treating it like it was no big deal. "You're in the safest place you can be."

"Cool," I said, nodding my head.

We stared uncomfortably at each other for several seconds, neither of us quite sure what to say next. Then, as if we'd orchestrated it, we burst out laughing in unison. We laughed so hard and for so long that we both had tears in our eyes. Here I had been experiencing all that indignation the day before, vilifying my own family, hating the world, contemplating taking my own life, and now I was in a psych unit laughing uncontrollably about my situation? It was the perfect psychotic moment. Years and years of pent-up negative emotions were being released at once and, strangely enough, through laughter. It felt like something scripted for Hollywood – another award-winning performance that would have won me a second Oscar – if only it were all a movie.

The best thing about that moment, though, was that the laughter was authentic. I no longer felt that I was a threat to harm myself. In fact, behind all of South Coast's checkpoints, security, and rules, ironically I felt a sense of freedom for the first time in years. I was no longer a prisoner in my own mind. I could be me, and I was going to be lodged with people just like me. The fury and frustration that consumed and controlled my mind less than twenty-four hours earlier was evaporating. Like others with suicidal thoughts, I did not want to die – I just wanted the pain to end. Though I hadn't been treated yet, I knew I was going to be, and that knowledge was enough to help me relax. I felt a sense of happiness that had eluded me for so long that I forgot what that feeling was like. I really believed things were going to be okay.

And it was all triggered by Mini's intervention.

Had she not stepped in when she did, would I have even made it out of my own bedroom alive? And if I had, would I have ever gotten help, or would I have just let the turmoil continue simmering in my head until I seriously hurt myself or someone else?

The first thing I learned very quickly at South Coast about depression, which had already been confirmed by Mini's actions, was that anyone suffering from depression cannot fight it alone. That's what I tried to do all of those years and why I failed so miserably to get control of my life. It is, in many ways, similar to a physical ailment. Anyone who breaks a bone or needs surgery or requires treatments for a disease cannot do it alone. They need help getting around, eating, dressing themselves, taking their medication. It takes a team effort to recover. Depression is no different.

The people at South Coast would teach me what depression is and help me realize, much to my surprise, that the seeds of my depression were planted during my high school years and began to infiltrate my life right after Herissa died in 1989. Nicole's gruesome death five years later exacerbated it, of course, as did all of the sideshows that followed her death: the rumors about her and our family, the spectacle of a criminal trial, and the media frenzy that made us prisoners in our own home. And in the years following all of that, anytime I felt like I was finally settling into a good place in my life, something else would happen that would set me back – Troy's death, and the collapse of my engagement, to name a couple – enabling the depression to keep such a tight grip on me that I felt I could not escape. It explained why, as I was about to swallow those pills the previous day, it was Nicole, Herissa, and Troy who were at the forefront of my mind. But just like so many times in the past, I dismissed that long-term pain and addressed the short-term issue of my failed engagement by trying to reconnect with my fiancé. I assumed that would solve my problems. I could not have been more wrong.

The Centers for Disease Control and Prevention list eight criteria for determining if someone may be suffering from depression:

- Having little interest or pleasure in doing things.
- Feeling down, depressed, or hopeless.
- Having trouble falling asleep or staying asleep, or sleeping too much.
- Having little energy or feeling tired.
- Having little appetite or overeating.
- Feeling bad about yourself or feeling that you were a failure, ultimately letting yourself or your family down.
- Struggling to concentrate on tasks at hand.
- Moving or speaking so slowly that other people notice, or being so restless that you are moving around a lot more than usual.

I dealt with all eight of those criteria at some point, but the South Coast staff also taught me that, no matter how many issues were contributing to my depression, it was absolutely possible to escape it. As difficult as that was to initially imagine, I learned that with hard work and resolve, I really could keep depression at bay for the rest of my life. But it had to begin with me accepting the fact that I needed help, something I had never before done. I had to admit that I was mentally ill and understand it was okay to acknowledge that, despite the stigma that existed with mental health issues. I had to admit I needed support – from a hospital, a specialist, a friend, a relative, a higher power, one of each, whomever. I could not go forward on this journey toward mental wellness alone.

To put it all in a nutshell: I had to stop fooling myself, stop pretending everything was okay, and start living a life of authenticity. No more happy face when I wasn't happy. No more pretending that I could simply push through depression on my own terms. No – Nicole, Herissa, and Troy were never coming back. But I had to learn how to come to terms with their deaths. There would be no closure; I don't believe you can ever find complete closure after suffering such heavy losses. But I had to learn to cope.

Cope – a key word in my recovery. How interesting it is to look back today on the verbal sparring match Denise and I had in the dining room during my breakdown and see how prophetic it was:

"You need coping skills!" Denise shouted.

"I don't have any!" I yelled back.

"Well you'd better find some!" she quickly snapped.

We were both right. I needed them, didn't have them, but had to find them. And the people at South Coast would help me do that. After spinning my wheels in mud for years, finally I was going to get some traction to try to liberate myself from depression's choke hold.

CHAPTER 4

BIG MAC, FRIES, AND A COKE

"I always felt like I had to be happy, happy, happy and never really reached out and got the spiritual, mental, physical, and emotional help I needed. I was taught to 'just get on with it,' and that brought me to the psych ward. I have been so debilitated and paralyzed. Absolutely exhausted. Not an exhaustion where you're so tired that you have to take a nap. An exhaustion that is more of 'I'm tired of the inner fight that I've got going on.' For the last few weeks I have been so angry and hateful and hurtful. Who have I become? Have I been lying to myself? Am I really a happy person?"

– My first journal entry at South Coast,
October 11, 2004

I spent ten ultra-intensive days at South Coast as an inpatient and more than two rigorous months as an outpatient, which lasted until my discharge on December 30, 2004. I participated in daily classes and group discussions, did a lot of comprehensive reading, filled out several worksheets, had many brief but generally fruitful visits from family members, and was given one-on-one time with doctors and trained staff – all to help me work through my problems.

I was also exposed to numerous tools for coping with depression, maybe none more instrumental in my healing than journaling. Keeping a personal diary of my thoughts and feelings was something I had done on my own on occasion in the years following Nicole's death. But I began journaling religiously as soon as I was admitted to South Coast, and I still journal regularly today. Journaling is more than just writing. In fact, being a good writer is not a prerequisite. Trust me, as I have reviewed my journals from my time at South Coast, so much of what I wrote was a convoluted mess – random thoughts, rambling, no sentence structure, angry on one line and happy on the next line, spelling and grammar errors galore.

But that's perfectly fine when journaling. There are no rules or grades for style. The purpose of journaling was to give me something I created and owned, to give me something of which I was in control. It was a way for me to express myself to myself in an honest manner whenever I wanted, an opportunity to say anything about anything or anybody whenever I felt like saying it, and without questions, judgments, or criticisms from outsiders. It was an outlet, a way to empty my mind and heart each day to try to make peace with myself and those who played a role in my life. And while it wasn't my intent at the time, a huge bonus was that it gave me something to reflect upon years later, to see what I was feeling and how I was progressing or regressing day to day – a good reminder of where I once was. It was an important piece of the puzzle toward my recovery.

That journal entry on October 11, 2004 was my first entry while at South Coast. I will share entries with you that I wrote during my nearly three months of therapy until the end of 2004 and in the first few months of 2005 when I re-entered the real world armed with a new lease on life. Reading that first entry today, I realize the "I was taught to 'just get on with it'" line perfectly defined how I had dealt with traumatic situations since my teen years. It's why it was second nature for me to always compartmentalize my problems, smile, and pretend everything was okay.

I was in high school in the mid-1980s when six of my classmates, all friends or acquaintances, suddenly and tragically lost their lives. Two were killed in hiking accidents. One passed away from leukemia. Two died in car wrecks. Another was killed in a skiing accident. I went to six funerals in four years. That was during an era when the primary responders to help students grieve in such heavy-hearted situations were academic counselors and teachers. They did the best they could to help us with our emotions, but that wasn't their expertise.

Nowadays, schools often have well-trained grief counselors and crisis teams, ready to go at a moment's notice, even on weekends if necessary. I don't remember us being encouraged to speak with somebody after each of the deaths at my school. There seemed to be no process in place to deal with the losses. It wasn't that my school was ignorant – it was that society was ignorant. Schools in general did not seem to take care of the emotional health of students very well, and nobody outside of schools recognized the problem enough to do something about it. We just went to the funerals, cried, said our goodbyes, consoled each other, and that was it. It was just a part of life. The next day we went back to class and moved on.

Herissa's death was the seventh and most difficult one I had to absorb in a six-year period. I met her in 1988 and we became instant best friends, practically joined at the hip, even though she was about seven years older than me. But a year later, after leaving a festival late one night, she was crossing a busy street in Laguna Beach just up the road from my house, and a car hit her and sped away. She died in the hospital the next day, and the person who killed her was never found. She was twenty-six years old.

I struggled with her death more than the previous ones for a couple of reasons: one was because she was my very best friend; the other was because she wanted me to go to the festival with her, but I didn't want to attend. Rather than just say that to her, I told her I had somewhere to be so as to not hurt her feelings. I lied. Maybe it was a small lie with the good intention of not making her feel bad, but when that's your last communication with a friend before parting ways with her forever, it eats at you day and night.

Our upbringings couldn't have been more different, but we deeply connected on an emotional level. Herissa was a spiritual being who believed in phenomena like the healing power of angels and dolphins. She was a wonderful soul who positively loved life. She had little money, yet I always looked at her as someone who had absolutely everything. Her presence was exotic and almost majestic. She welcomed people of all backgrounds, races, and faiths into her harmonious world, instantly loving them all unconditionally. She was happy all the time, one of those people who just got what life is supposed to be about. Having "stuff" didn't matter to her. She believed life was about something or someone far greater than anything or anyone we could ever find on this planet, which made her a peaceful, worry-free person. I loved her and admired her profoundly for that sentiment.

I was so fixated on Herissa's death that I could not let her go no matter how hard I tried. One thing I've learned over the years is that dealing with the deaths of people you love is one of those rare aspects of life that does not get easier with experience. Each one hurts as much as, or more than, the previous one. Despite losing all of those classmates in high school and finding a way to push forward after each one, I could not mentally overcome Herissa's tragic end.

> *"Before Herissa died, I had been taught to not allow the death of a loved one to drag you down. You have to control it and accept it. I could not do that with Herissa."*
>
> – November 18, 2004

The depression triggered by her loss oozed into every part of my brain and even affected me physically. I was attending Orange Coast College at the time of her death, and it was a battle the next two years to simply get out of bed in the morning. When I did attend my classes, I smiled and pretended everything was fine. But behind the scenes, it was ugly. There were no smiles. Some days I literally could not move when I woke up. I was paralyzed, spending a lot of time on the couch with the lights out and curtains drawn. I could not find the will to do anything.

I remember my mom telling me I looked very gray, like I'd aged twenty years in a matter of weeks. I had the joy, the life, everything sucked right out of me. Mom tried to motivate me by posting affirmations around the house. I would find phrases like "You are strong" written on a sticky note on my pillow, or "You can overcome this" stuck to the bathroom door. She bought me a beautiful plant with a card full of encouraging words. Bless her heart for trying, but it was futile. I was totally null and void.

The lack of motivation to do anything included eating. Getting my butt off the couch to walk the twenty feet to the refrigerator was too exhausting to even think about. And when I did conjure up the energy to make the trek, about all I could digest was apple sauce, cottage cheese, and salsa. I know – gross. Don't try that combo. I did so little eating in the days and weeks after Herissa's funeral that I dropped several pounds I really could not afford to lose. At 5 feet 10 inches tall and already slender, I didn't have to avoid food for too long to look physically ill.

Mom gently tried to coax me into eating by placing various foods in front of me. If I were on the couch watching television, she'd try to hook me by discreetly sliding a bowl of chips or fruit on the coffee table in front of me, hoping I'd be like a fish and lunge at the bait. But I would ignore it. Then she would up the ante by going out and returning with a Big Mac and fries, hoping the aroma would elicit a response. My response was normally a sprint to the bathroom to vomit. She eventually tried to use force, attempting to shove apple slices down my throat, clenching my jaw with her hands to try to make me chew. I fought her like she was trying to make me ingest arsenic. I won, if you want to consider that a victory.

"You need to eat, Tanya," she repeated over and over, only to have it fall upon deaf ears. Out of ideas, Mom finally left me alone, praying and hoping that I would come around with time, though she knew time was not an ally.

I don't know how Mom was able to watch me do that to myself, but her patience and prayers were finally answered after a few weeks when I woke up one morning and had an epiphany. I gazed at myself in the mirror as I was getting dressed and wasn't sure who I was anymore. I could not believe how awful I looked.

Wow, Tanya, what are you doing to yourself? I thought, recognizing for the first time that my ribs and shoulder blades were hideously disrupting the flow of my once-smooth skin. It was the first time I could see the reason for Mom's urgency that I eat: I looked like someone trying to slowly kill herself. Was that what I was trying to do? No, at least not consciously. That's when I realized how right Mom was. I *did* need to eat, and I *could* overcome this. I felt horrible for putting Mom through all that I did and, though it still wasn't easy, I knew I needed to climb out of my funk and start eating something more. I began that day with small bits of assorted foods such as a piece of bread, a morsel of chocolate, and some fruit, even moving my jaw without her help when consuming apple slices.

Having hit such a low with almost no food in me for several weeks, it took a little while for my taste buds and stomach to adjust, but once they did, I gained a new appreciation for food. I was infused with energy I hadn't had in a long time. As the days rolled along, a piece of bread turned into loaves, a morsel turned into chunks, and slices turned into batches. I started to eat a little more. And a little more. And a little more. And a lot more. And then a whole lot more.

As crazy and improbable as it may sound, considering I had been perfectly content with the apple sauce/cottage cheese/salsa trifecta, I started eating everything in sight. I went from one extreme to the other, from hardly eating and being rail thin to overeating and packing on the pounds like I was storing food for winter. I was overeating, binge eating, hoarding. It was similar to someone going from never taking a drink in her life to rounding up every bottle of liquor she could find and becoming an alcoholic in a couple of week's time. This became my new way of coping with depression, and it spun out of control.

> *"I began to eat everything in sight. My food became my shelter, my escape, my refuge. I became a closet eater, chowing down two breakfasts, two lunches, and two dinners every day without anyone really knowing what I was doing."*
>
> – October 18, 2004

Mom would set dinner on the table and I'd literally attack it with my fork. Have you ever seen the movie *Parental Guidance* when Billy Crystal bought a sheet cake for his grandchildren whose mother, Marisa Tomei, had never let them have sugar before? They looked like they'd just emerged from battle after devouring it. I was those grandkids. I claimed my share of food, plus a little of everyone else's. Mini recalled me shoveling my dinner down each night like it was an Olympic event, which I always effortlessly won, then silently drooling over everyone else's food.

"You were eyeing my food like a vicious dog," she told me years later, always fearful that I was going to snatch it away from her. "I had to eat faster so that you wouldn't take it."

There was always a wild party going on in my stomach. After dinner, I'd invade the pantry or fridge and eat some more, continually going back until it was time to go to bed. Cookies, ice cream, crackers, cold cuts, whatever; everything was fair game. And then when I went to bed, I'd eat. I'd pull my pajamas out of my dresser drawer, along with a couple bags of chips. I kept a stash of food under the bed and in my nightstand drawers. Boxes and bags of food were everywhere. I hid food in my coat pockets. In the garage. In my car. No matter where I was, I could always count on there being something edible. If I ran out of anything, I rushed to the grocery store and replenished. Food is what made me happy, superficially anyway. It was my crutch and was holding me up pretty darn well.

I even took it another ridiculous step by inadvertently making a mockery of weight-loss guru Jenny Craig. I had pushed my weight to an unprecedented 195 pounds, and my shrinking clothes enlightened me to the fact that I was now becoming unhealthy to the other extreme. While loafing on the couch one afternoon, I saw one of Jenny Craig's commercials and decided to try her program, which required eating her special food. Lose weight by eating good food? How could I beat that? I ordered it and stuck to it for a while, eating nothing but the food she recommended. The end result, however, was one that probably few people on her program have ever done – I gained weight. The food was so tasty to me that I scarfed down way too much of it. Every shipment of it I received was like Christmas morning. Sad? Oh yeah. I totally abused her system and became addicted to all of her meals and snacks. After the first few days, I didn't even attempt to follow her diet plan. I had to have been one of her best customers and worst examples at the same time. I had no self-control.

If somebody invited me to lunch at noon, it was not uncommon for me to eat breakfast that morning, usually twice, then leave early for lunch so that I could swing by McDonald's and pick up a combo meal to eat in the car on the way. Yes, I would stop at McDonald's for lunch on my way to lunch and right after breakfast. The food my mom unsuccessfully tried to get me to eat when I refused to eat was now my anchor. Nothing topped the combo meal – a Big Mac, large fries, and large Coke.

One time I was on my way to a birthday party where I knew there was going to be a lot of food served, yet I stopped at McDonald's on the way. Just before I got to the party, I threw the trash out the window. I felt horribly guilty for littering, so much so that it still bothers me today. But at the time, it was all about hiding the evidence. That's what food wrappers, crumbs, and bags had become to me: evidence. Sure, people could see I was gaining weight, but how I was doing it was embarrassing. I didn't want anybody to find out.

Fortunately, though, Mom finally did figure it out.

Noticing the stack of plates in her kitchen cupboard was shrinking, she went into my room one day to see what she could find. Much to her chagrin, she found far more than she had hoped: dirty plates under the bed, food everywhere, crumbs on the sheets. I'm surprised there weren't any rats hanging out. They were probably afraid I'd eat them, too.

"Oh my," she said to me, holding a grimy plate with dried sauce or dried something on it. I dropped my head, the guilt of a little kid whose hand was caught in the cookie jar shrouding me. "What has happened to my little girl?"

Later that evening, Mom told Dad what she found.

"Why are you letting yourself go like this?" he said to me with a direct, yet sympathetic tone. And just like that, I ended the indulgence cold turkey and got myself back on a normal eating cycle. I was fortunate that I was able to shift my eating habits that quickly and easily, but it was unfortunate that it always seemed to take something shocking for me to change. When I wasn't consuming enough, I didn't start eating until I finally recognized how awful my body looked. When I was eating too much, I didn't reduce my intake until my dad made that comment. You see, Dad usually took a back seat to Mom when it came to dealing with us kids. So when he did speak up, I listened.

Chapter 5

Accept Whatever Life Deals You

"I think if my parents were to die today, given the lack of sharing my life with my dad, I would probably flip out again. Mom and I speak about life on a daily basis. But as for Dad, I sometimes feel like I don't really know him. I don't have the peace that he is at peace. I want to share my heart with my dad and let him know how proud I am of him. I sometimes wonder how he can be proud of me. I haven't been successful. I never finished college. He lost two kids – one to murder, and another (from a previous marriage) five years earlier to ALS. The life of this man – how can he be proud of me?

"I not only want to be a success in my life for me, but also to share that success for him. I am so mad and disappointed in myself that I didn't listen to my dad more when I was in high school. What's done is done. I'm just happy he came to see me in the hospital. Mom and I have our own little agreement. But for Daddy to come was huge. I was so happy he did. I have such a warm place in my heart for my dad."

– November 6, 2004

My parents, Lou and Juditha, are the two most selfless, kindest, and strongest people I have ever had the pleasure of knowing. Sure, most of us probably think that of our parents. But trying to look at them objectively, I don't know two other people I'd rather have in my corner. The qualities they possess can be traced back to their upbringings, traits they've tried

45

hard to instill into their children and grandchildren. They are, and always have been, "old school," trusting in their morals and values to guide them through every complex situation.

Prior to Nicole's murder, we were as normal as any family anywhere, with "family" truly being the heart of who we were. Holidays, birthdays, vacations, walks along the beach – we were always doing something together, even as we girls got older. After the murder, it took time to regain some semblance of that normalcy, but we have, in many respects, managed to do so. And all of the credit goes to our parents, who never wavered from their principles.

My father, a native of California, was born in 1923 and served as a captain in the U.S. Army Air Corps. He flew B-17 bombers during World War II and was honorably discharged after the war with several medals, including the American Campaign Medal, Army of Occupation Medal, and World War II Victory Medal.

He was married and had three children before he and his wife divorced. She and one of their daughters both died of ALS, or Lou Gehrig's disease. The daughter, with whom Dad had a good relationship, died in 1989. He is also close with his other two children from that marriage. To my sisters and me, they have always been part of our extended family.

I have a very good relationship with my dad, though as I said in the journal entry at the start of this chapter, I often wondered how proud I made him. It wasn't so obvious to me when I was young and naïve, but as I grew older, I finally learned to appreciate all of the many propitious characteristics he has tried to impart to me. Look at the life he has lived – sacrificing himself by fighting for his country in World War II, having seven children, finding the fortitude to live through the heartbreaking deaths of two of his daughters, financially supporting his family with businesses he courageously started on his own. And while we may not be perfect children, I think we came out pretty darn good. It took me a while, but I now understand the level of love my father has always had for us. He may not have said it every day, but he has certainly shown it in the way he has lived his life.

I think a perfect example of the strength and integrity my dad has can be found in an interview he, my mom, and Denise did with TV journalist Diane Sawyer in October 1995 on the day O.J. was exonerated of Nicole's murder. Ms. Sawyer asked what would happen to Nicole and O.J.'s two young children, Sydney, who was going to be ten years old in a few weeks, and Justin, who was seven. This was my dad's response, despite the fact that he had a strong suspicion the children's father killed Nicole:

"Our grandchildren now have a father that's a free man, whereas they have no mother … but at least they have one parent to back up their life," he said. "I've stated in the past that I would (fight for the children) … but we gain nothing by fighting. Infighting in the family is never healthy. The kids would suffer, and that's the main thing we want to avoid."

Total class.

While his strength is immeasurable, behind every strong man is a strong woman, as the old saying goes, and that's Mom – the other half of that fabulous team. A native of Germany and seven years younger than my dad, she met him after the war when they were both working in Germany at *Stars and Stripes* newspaper.

"I was standing at the bus station one day when he drove slowly past me," Mom recalled to me, about ready to laugh. "He wouldn't take his eyes off me – and he ended up crashing right into another car!" A small price to pay since he eventually asked her out and married her. For several years they remained in Germany, where Denise and Nicole were born, before moving to California. They had four girls, have lived in the same modest ranch home for forty years, and will celebrate their fifty-eighth wedding anniversary in 2014. Dad worked in the insurance business after the war before becoming an entrepreneur – owning a car repair shop and, eventually, a car wash business. While Dad was the primary breadwinner, Mom was our primary caretaker.

I go back to the term "old school" to describe Mom. She was a traditional stay-at-home mother who got us to school every day, cooked our meals, helped us with homework, and even sewed our clothes. She also worked part time as a travel agent. She was born and raised Catholic and raised us in the same faith.

"Being a war child, I was brought up by parents who were strong in character and strong in faith," Mom told me. "You accepted whatever life dealt you and believed that God would not give you more than you could carry."

She has proven that day in and day out over the course of my life. Not only did she lose a daughter in the most heinous way, but she has survived cancer twice, including a lumpectomy and nearly forty radiation treatments while in her 80s, never wavering in her positive attitude. During those treatments, she never stopped taking care of my dad who has had Alzheimer's disease the past couple of years and needs constant care. After Nicole was killed, Mom, while in her early 60s, basically became a mother to two young children – Sydney and Justin. She was such an influence on them that she still receives phone calls from both of them each week, even though they are adults now and living on the other side of the country.

The courts granted us visitation rights with the kids. When it was our family's time to have them, we somehow had to make the transfer with their father. Sometimes he would send the children over with a driver. Sometimes he would bring them himself. Other times Mom would have to go to his house to pick them up. Imagine having to do this time and time again with the man you believe killed your daughter. One day, Mom asked me if I would go pick them up because she was trying to get some other things done before the kids came over. The thought made me sick.

"But Mom, what if I have to go into the house?" I said.

"Then you go into the house," she replied. "You are there for those kids. Leave all opinions at the door."

I did as she asked. When I got there, the kids came running outside to me and jumped into my arms. Their father followed them and offered his hand to shake mine. I looked at it – but just couldn't do it. I opted to give him a pat on the back.

"Where is their luggage?" I asked, anxious to get away.

"It's inside," he said. I reluctantly followed him in and felt nauseous the second we walked in the door. There were furnishings that once belonged to Nicole, most of which she picked out herself to decorate the place. My heart raced. My skin was sweaty and clammy. The whole house was fermenting with negative energy. I got the luggage, the kids, and out of there as fast as I could.

As I pulled away from the house, I had a new appreciation for my mom. Not that I needed one; she was already my hero. But imagine what kind of woman it takes to be able to do what she did for those kids all those years. Absolutely amazing.

Just prior to Mom receiving her chemotherapy treatments during her first bout with cancer, I talked with her about what she was going to go through. I was afraid of the unknown and asked her if she was scared. She had shown no sign of being frightened in the least since her diagnosis.

"Scared about what?" she said. Like everything from Mom's lips, she was being totally honest with her answer. She never once listened to any of the doubts people tried to put in her mind about cancer. She never listened to comments about how the treatment was going to negatively affect her life. If someone said something that she thought might bring her down, she closed her ears. That attitude wasn't just to help herself get through it for her own sake; she was doing it for my dad, who she knew needed her. With the ability and intelligence and altruism to think like that, it's very easy to understand her response: "Scared about what?"

My mom is someone who does what has to be done for the good of her family. If you see her today, despite all she has been through, she looks about ten to twenty years younger than she is, an outer beauty that I believe stems from her inner beauty – one of peace and love toward everyone with whom she comes in contact. Generally, if you meet her once, you have a friend for life.

I don't think the picture I've painted of my parents is a very exciting one, which is exactly how they would like it. Despite what tabloids or other media may have depicted my parents to be over the years since Nicole's death, be it out for money or seeking attention, my parents are the absolute opposite. Mom and Dad are truly quiet, humble, hard-working, middle-class people who try to make the most of each day. They are two people who, I believe, deserve the utmost respect for what they have accomplished and have been through in their lives.

Just a few days after I checked into South Coast, I wrote my parents a letter. While most of the writing I did there was personal journaling, this letter to Mom and Dad meant the most to me out of everything I wrote because they mean the most to me. After all they'd suffered throughout their lives, the last thing they needed was more despair involving one of their children. By writing this letter to them, I not only assured them that I was going to work hard at straightening out my life, but I placed the pressure on myself to follow through with that promise to them. I did not, under any circumstance, want to let them down. Here it is, in its entirety:

Mama & Daddy,

The night time is always so hard for me, but I wanted to write a letter to you in pencil (cuz they don't give you any pens. I guess a pen could do more damage). I really like my days here. I feel productive. The classes are incredible. I am asking the teachers how to apply this stuff in your darkest and saddest moments. They have answers. It's gonna be hard, but I'm gonna try. It's scary. I cry a lot and today was asked if I could erase one word. I chose hate. I don't like the word and it's been eating me up. I don't want you to think this is your fault or anything. It is truly all my losses of friends, relationships, O.J., Nicole ... all of it is contributing to it. I guess I'm not as strong as I wish I could be. But look where it put me – in the psych ward at South Coast.

I am sorry I have put you through this. But I know at the end I will be a little better than before. I am very embarrassed about the other evening, but it was a blessing because it gave me help that I need. Please forgive me for being such an embarrassment to the family on that evening. I wasn't drunk, but my anger, rage, and depression had its fill. I love you guys a lot and know you're supporting me being here.

Here are my 5 good thoughts/things that happened to-day:

- *I smiled to an unexpected compliment.*
- *I saw a butterfly outside my window.*
- *I got a lot of good information from my classes.*
- *I saw a movie.*
- *Mini came with gifts, clothes and pictures.*

And thank you for the writing paper. Nights around here are sad and lonely so that is why I am going to sleep now. I love you both.

— Tanya

Chapter 6

Some Things Just Are

"I always felt like I had to follow in the footsteps of my sisters, and that I was letting people down if I didn't. They were all beautiful and popular. Nicole was married to the pro football player. Denise was a model and on the cover of Cosmopolitan in the 1970s. Dominique not only was gorgeous, but was at the top of her high school class academically. All of them were on their homecoming courts. And then there was me – a tall, lanky kid who really didn't have the physical beauty they had, and always struggled in school. Nobody said I should be more like them, but I always felt like that comparison was there, and I wasted a lot of time wanting what they had instead of just being me."

– October 13, 2004

Yes, I felt my sisters had everything – beauty, brains, popularity – all of which I believed I did not have growing up, at least at their levels. I placed undue pressure on myself to emulate them, even concocting a bit of a rivalry with each of them inside my own mind. But gradually, most notably after my therapy, I found my own voice and realized I needed to be Tanya and nobody else. That also led to more positive and rewarding relationships with Mini and Denise after my therapy.

Mini is five years older than me, much closer to my age than Denise or Nicole. While growing up, it was usually Denise and Nicole hanging out together, and Mini and me doing our own thing. If I could describe Mini in one word, it would be that she is a "doer." In the same respect as my mom, when something has to get done, you can count on Mini to do it, and to do it efficiently. She has worked various jobs over the years, many of those as an executive assistant, which is right up her alley.

When Nicole died, and with everybody's heads spinning in a state of shock, Mini took over the difficult tasks and details that nobody wanted to do, or knew how to do. She picked out Nicole's clothes, her jewelry, the casket. Nobody asked her to. It just needed to be done, so she did it. It was natural for her and was probably her way of dealing with the grief of losing her sister. She reacted in the same manner toward me when I melted down in front of my family in 2004.

> *"I needed that one weekend of drinking and popping those pills to get me into the hospital. Mini making the call for me and just flat out calling the insurance company, calling the hospital for a room, and just taking charge – it literally saved my life."*
>
> – October 29, 2004

I wonder to this day what would have happened if Mini hadn't taken me to Deana's parents' house and then to South Coast. She said she knew nobody else was going to step up and take me. It wasn't necessarily that they didn't want to, but they didn't know to. Mental illness was foreign to everyone in my family, including me. But Mini, who had her share of personal struggles in dealing with Nicole's death, realized what was happening, knew how grave the situation was, and how much worse it could become.

"I knew something needed to be done, and it wasn't a bandage or a pill you needed – you needed serious help," Mini told me years later. "I'd never seen anyone act that way before, and I knew you were about to become destructive."

Mini didn't just drop me off at South Coast, but she stayed by my side until I was checked in, visited me on a daily basis while I was there, and even attended some of my group therapy sessions. No, we haven't had a perfect relationship our entire lives. Just like any sisters, we've had our struggles, our arguments, our disagreements, our silly fights, but she has always been there for me when I have needed her most, and usually without me having to ask.

Denise, who is twelve years older than me ... well, I'm glad I can smile and laugh when I reflect on the relationship we've had. It has definitely had its turbulent times, but I'm happy to say our friendship today is the happiest and strongest it has ever been.

In 2004, though ...

> *"I wrote a letter of apology to Denise. It said something like 'I now realize that my words have hurt you. I wasn't in my right frame of mind (on Oct. 9). I don't remember half the stuff I said. I hope you can find it in your heart to forgive me.' She &*#%*$@ rips me! She says she doesn't believe me when I say I don't remember certain things. She judged me. She said I feel sorry for myself. Oh, okay, I think I will throw myself into a &*#%*$@ mental hospital so people feel &*#%*$@ sorry for me. I will pop pills so people feel sorry for me. Come on Denise, get real."*
>
> *– November 14, 2004*

And that was just a sliver of the anger I penned toward her. For every handful of pages in my journals that I wrote at South Coast about other issues bothering me, there was a page ranting about Denise. My hostility toward her stemmed from her assertiveness to deal with the media on behalf of our family after Nicole's death, from her taking charge of the Nicole Brown Charitable Foundation that our parents started to combat domestic violence, and from her excluding me – or so I felt – from all of it. While I still do not agree with the way she handled everything back then, I have a better grasp today of how Denise perceived herself and me at that time.

I was just twenty-four years old when Nicole died, had lived at home most of my life with little real-world experience, and I was already suffering through depression (from Herissa's death) that I failed to acknowledge. Not exactly a slam-dunk résumé for being put in charge of anything. Denise, meanwhile, was thirty-six. She had traveled the world as a fashion model while developing strong leadership skills. Now she was dealing with the loss of not only her sister, but of a sister who was her dearest and closest friend, making the loss a little more personal for her. When they were younger, it was always Denise and Nicole teamed up against the world. If one of them liked you or didn't like you, could count on the other one feeling the exact same way. They were inseparable.

Denise also couldn't shake a perception she had of me – that of the "little princess." All of my sisters often called me that when I was a kid, saying I was the spoiled, youngest child who got whatever she wanted from Mommy and Daddy by throwing tantrums. I will admit there was definitely some truth to that. I felt it was the only way I could snag some attention from my parents in a house where attention was oftentimes at a premium. But Denise still had that "little princess" perception of me into adulthood. So when I had my mental breakdown in 2004, she looked at it as Tanya crying wolf again – throwing a tantrum for attention, and nothing too serious to worry about.

> *"OK, I know I am not a 'purrfect' angel. I have been coddled my whole life, but at 35, I am now waking up. I really have not lived out my own life. I have been living out everyone's perception of how to live. The baby princess. The spoiled brat. It's all &*#%$@*! I am done. In the past, I used to feel sorry for myself because I felt it was the only way to be heard in this family as the baby girl. But the perception everyone has of me now is a child comparison to my adult life. That was twenty years ago! Ya think I may have changed a lot since then?"*
>
> *– November 27, 2004*

You can clearly see my confusion in that journal entry, admitting that I had been coddled my whole life and was just waking up to it at thirty-five years old, but then a few sentences later claiming that I had certainly changed from twenty years earlier. With that battle of who I really was being fought in my own mind, and considering who others thought I was, it's easy to understand why Denise and I were still at odds with each other well into our adult lives.

Our relationship finally took a positive turn about a year after my breakdown, and I think something we each learned about the other is what contributed to it.

The new perspective I gained about Denise was that she grieved very differently than I did about Nicole's death, which didn't make her way wrong, just different – something I didn't grasp at the time. Denise was always very open and blunt about how she felt about O.J.'s role in it, believing without a doubt that he killed Nicole. She never hid her emotions about how much it hurt to lose Nicole. She took the lead role in the foundation not only to change something horrific into something good for women around the world who were victims of domestic violence, but also to help herself heal. I, on the other hand, bottled up everything, kept my opinions to myself, and stayed in the background as I felt everybody wanted me to do. I worried more about pretending to be happy instead of taking care of me. Our polar opposite ways of dealing with the loss of Nicole eventually came to a head.

What Denise learned about my situation was that she did not understand mental illness and that the brain really could just snap. Her brain didn't function that way, even though she was closer to Nicole than I was, so why should mine? Though she may come across to some as a cruel person for rejecting the apology letter I sent her from South Coast, I realize now that she wasn't cruel at all. Like many people, she just didn't get it, which is why today there is still that stigma attached to mental illness. Denise wasn't trying to be hurtful. She was simply uneducated about my tribulations, and it took her a while to figure that out and accept it. Once she understood my illness, and once I took the time to understand what she had gone through, our relationship began to mend, and now it flourishes today.

While we no longer have the foundation due to time constraints and new directions we all took in our lives, Denise passionately continues her crusade against domestic violence in other ways – by hosting a weekly Internet show on social issues at dtalksradio.com and through her ownership of The Elite Speakers Bureau, a group of about three dozen speakers with a mission to bring about social change in various capacities. I am one of those speakers and, with Denise's help, am gradually joining her as the face of the Brown family on those important issues with which I once felt she did not want me involved.

Nicole, the second-oldest among the four of us, was ten years older than me, but we were much closer than that age difference would indicate. She loved to be a big sister, taking me shopping or on weekend road trips. She gave me advice about life when she felt I could use it. She invited me to her house often when I was older for no reason other than just to visit. The way she treated me, though, was a microcosm of what meant the most to her: family. And when you walked into her home, you knew it.

You knew it by the happiness in the eyes and voices of her children. You knew it by the way she treated her husband, despite the way we later found out he was treating her. You could literally see it on her walls, which were plastered with family photos. She loved taking pictures – so much so that after she was killed, it was difficult to find any photos of her to pay tribute because she was always the one taking the photos. She would get them developed right away, write a caption on them, matte and frame them, and give them as gifts or hang them in her home. When she died, she left behind eighty photo albums.

Nicole's creative mind led her to work as an interior decorator for part of her life, and she was darn good at it. She had a knack for fashion and the latest trends, and she had impeccable taste. She could turn gloom into glamour with little effort.

Yes, she had nice "things" because her husband was a professional football player who made a lot of money during his career, but she could have and would have given it all up in a heartbeat if she had to. She drove a Ferrari, but treated it like a station wagon. If you climbed into the back seat, you'd find week-old French fries crushed between the seats and plastic

Happy Meal toys scattered on the floor. She was an average Jane who had money, but never flaunted it, never let it define who she was, and never lost sight of what was important in life.

Nicole divorced O.J. in 1992 and, for the last couple years of her life, she enjoyed her freedom from the years of violence she had endured. She loved to host parties and enjoyed going to parties when she could. The good company was what mattered to her. But after she died, many negative things were said about her that simply weren't true – that she was excessive in her partying and a drug user – all in an effort by certain media to create scoops and higher ratings.

> *"Nicole was not the 'party girl' that she was made out to be. She was my big sister, a very understanding woman who put everyone else in front of her. She was a giver. People who didn't know Nicole saw her as a big partier who was always all dolled up. I saw her as a beach girl with cutoff shorts, bikini top, flip-flops, chewing gum, and playing with her kids. Her last days were not partying days, as many people reported. They were suffering days of fighting off pneumonia, and attending her daughter's dance recital, and having dinner with the family. That's who she was. In so many ways, she was my inspiration."*
>
> – October 27, 2004

The most memorable inspiration she bestowed upon me was on Christmas Eve in 1993, the day before the last Christmas she and I would ever spend together. I had been going to college since the fall at the University of California San Diego and was at my apartment there early that afternoon. While I probably should have been on the road making the ninety-minute drive home for Christmas, I was instead drinking wine and watching the movie *Casablanca* with the curtains closed and lights out. How sad is that? I was bummed about school, which was not going well, and I could not mentally overcome it. I was attending classes, studying hard, but still failing. After Herissa's death, the weight loss, and the weight gain, this was an extension of the depression for which I'd failed to get help. I was so despondent that I was thinking about quitting school before the next semester started after break.

I was about halfway into the movie when the phone rang. It was Nicole.

"Hey girl, what's up?" she asked.

"Not much," I said glumly.

"You don't sound too good. Mom tells me that you're really unhappy," she said.

"Nic, I'm just not doing well," I said, "and I don't know why. I want to be here. I'm trying. But I'm just not getting it when I'm in class."

We talked about the classes for a little while before she told me to go get a pen and paper.

"I want you to write down a saying I always use, something you can keep with you for when you need it," she said.

"OK," I said, wondering what words of wisdom she was going to give me that I would probably discard with the wine bottle once it was empty. I just wasn't in the mood for a cliché quote from a famous person that she found in a magazine or book. But the words turned out to be all hers.

"Here it is," she said. "Delete the need to understand. We don't need to understand everything. Some things just are."

To this day, I share that quote in every presentation I give on mental health. It is so simple, so general, but I have found it makes perfect sense in almost every aspect of our lives. In every journal entry I made as a patient at South Coast, I asked many questions of myself and others in an attempt to figure out everything in my life. It's good to ask questions. It's good to be curious. It's good to wonder. It's good to search for answers. But when all the answers aren't revealed, we can't drive ourselves insane worrying about it. The simple fact is that we aren't going to figure out everything. And we don't need to.

You may be familiar with the *Serenity Prayer*: "God, grant me the serenity to accept the things I cannot change; courage to change the things I can; and wisdom to know the difference." I learned at South Coast that once we take that attitude with those things that are beyond our control, a burden is lifted from our minds, which can be the difference between suffering from depression and living a life full of happiness.

> *"I know Nicole's in a safe place now, a place where she is able to breathe and live just like she wanted to – this is one of the things I say to myself to keep my strength. Heaven is a place free of anger, sadness, worry, and anxiety. I live every day knowing she is here in spirit, but she will never be back physically. I miss her more than anything else."*
>
> – October 27, 2004

I will obviously never forget what happened to Nicole, or how it happened. I will never forget the endless pain we all experienced at the time and still deal with today. Her birthday and the anniversary of her death have been, and will always be, haunting every year. But I've learned to manage it. I've learned that, with help, it really is possible to move forward, even without forgetting. One way I've learned to do that is by applying her own words to her inexplicable death: some things just are.

CHAPTER 7

THAT'S MY KID

"The pain is not exterior. It is the pain of an empty heart. A heart that has a huge hole in it. A heart that will never be the same because something is missing. This is what I have to see every day. I pray for all families around the world that they never have to go through this. Pray that your parents go before you do, because nothing is worse than suffering the loss of a child."

— October 28, 2004

From the deaths of my high school classmates and Herissa, to my eating disorders, to my academic struggles in college, I had plenty of reasons to be depressed in the early 1990s, especially considering I didn't seek the professional help back then that I needed for all of that adversity. But none of those afflictions came close to matching the grief I experienced from losing my sister. Nicole was just thirty-five, had two young children, and died in the most dreadful and unimaginable way possible.

To say I sunk deeper into depression because of her death is a very true, but very broad, statement. It wasn't just her death, but countless incidents associated with it, such as witnessing my parents' reaction to finding out their child died, watching our once normal and private lives unfold publicly through the media, hearing helicopters hovering over our home, seeing TV satellite trucks parked across the street every day trying to capture our every move, and walking through Nicole's condo just two days after she was killed. Even little things that may appear insignificant to the average person had a gut-wrenching impact on me, such as when I found in her condo a cup of melted ice cream she'd bought minutes before she was killed.

There were conversations I had with her around the time of her messy divorce that I reflected upon with horrendous guilt, conversations in which I felt I should have read between the lines and realized she was being abused and needed help. Over time those incidents and reflections mounted in my mind, completely consuming my being. I thought I could deal with it all. I thought I *was* dealing with it all. But I wasn't. I couldn't. And it eventually caught up with me to the point where ten years later I was so overwhelmed that I nearly took my own life.

The news of Nicole's death on the evening of June 12, 1994, did not reach our home until the next morning. It was about 6:30 A.M., and I was sound asleep in my room at the far end of the house. Though the vibrant sun was already forty-five minutes into its day and trying to fight its way through my window, the drawn shades kept me concealed in darkness. It was a Monday, a workday, and I still had about a half hour before I needed to get ready. I wasn't budging. I had planned to milk every minute of sleep I could.

But then ... the screams.

"Noooooo!! My God!! No!! No!! Noooo!!"

They were horrendous, painful, earsplitting shrieks that will be forever ingrained in my memory. I threw my covers off, jumped up, slung the bedroom door open, and dashed into Sean's room, which was right next to mine. Sean, Denise's son, was just seven years old. My first instinct was that he may have been having a bad dream, but it wasn't him I heard. It was Denise.

"What's going on?" I said, attempting to adjust my tired eyes to the bright bedroom light. Denise was sitting on the edge of the bed, hunched over, tightly squeezing Sean against her chest. Her face was soaked with tears.

"She's dead!" Denise cried, rocking Sean back and forth. "She's dead!"

She's dead? What on earth … ?

"Who's dead?" I asked, bewildered.

"Coco!" she screamed.

"Coco?"

"Yes! Coco! Your sister!" That was the nickname some of the kids in the family had given Nicole. I knew that – I knew she was talking about Nicole, but it still wasn't registering.

"What do you mean she's dead?" I asked. "You were just with her last night. She can't be dead."

"*Yes!* She's *dead!*" Denise said emphatically, becoming irritated with my denial. "He killed her! Coco's dead!"

I heard her say, "He killed her," but didn't really listen, giving no thought whatsoever to whom "He" was. Having been awakened so abruptly, I was still not fully cognizant of what was going on. I knew Denise and the rest of my family were with Nicole the previous night, probably not even ten hours earlier, at a dance recital for Sydney. After that, they went out to dinner at Mezzaluna near Nicole's condo before going back to their respective homes. I was awake when they got home that evening, and I remember everybody being happy, talking about what a good time they had. How could she be dead? That didn't make any sense.

Still in a fog, and now even more confused after hearing Denise's erratic claims, I tentatively made my way down the hallway and toward the dining room where I could see a light was on. When I walked in, I found my mom sitting at the table by herself. Her elbows were leaning on it with the palms of her hands pressed against her cheeks, her fingers covering her eyes. Something was obviously wrong. *My God,* I thought, becoming more alert after seeing her demeanor. *What is happening?*

"Mom?" I said hesitantly. She didn't move.

"Mom? Denise said something happened to Nicole."

Still no reaction.

"Mom?" She slowly slid her fingers down from her eyes, keeping them over her nose and mouth. She had a dreadful look of despair. I feared asking again.

"Mom … is it true?"

She covered her eyes again and gently nodded. I would find out later that she had just received a phone call about it a few minutes earlier from Detective Tom Lange with the Los Angeles Police Department.

"What? How?" I cried, raising my voice to the level of Denise's a minute earlier. I still couldn't fathom any of this. It was like I was walking in a bad dream, but I couldn't wake up. This all had to be a mistake, some kind of miscommunication.

"Mom, where's Daddy?" I asked. She didn't answer, which terrified me to no end. I'd never seen her like this. I ran past her and through the living room toward their bedroom on the other side of the house, my heart racing faster than my feet could move.

"Daddy? Daddy?" I called in a panic. I burst into their bedroom. He wasn't in bed. Without stopping, I kept going toward the bathroom, where the light was on and the door was partially open. I shoved it all the way open, and there he was – in a scene that will forever be rooted in my mind. He was leaning over the sink, his head hanging. One hand was smashed flat on the counter supporting all of his weight, the other one clenched and pounding that same counter over and over. He was sobbing, something I'd only seen him do once in my twenty-four years of life – when his daughter from his previous marriage died five years earlier from her long illness.

"Daddy? Oh God ... is it true?"

He never looked up. I was completely stunned.

"Yes," he said in a groggy voice, barely able to spit the word out. My throat immediately started to close as I lost my breath and burst into tears. I threw my arms around him, and we wept bitterly for what seemed like forever. Time stood still. No more words were exchanged. We just held each other and let our emotions go. What else could we do?

That, right there, was the worst pain and saddest moment I have ever experienced in my life. Not just finding out for certain that my sister was dead, but seeing my parents, firsthand, suffer through the excruciating agony and grief of learning that one of their children was gone. It was a feeling of hopelessness, a situation in which I could neither do nor say anything to comfort them.

Nicole didn't die of old age. She didn't die of a long-term illness. She was killed by another person. It wasn't her time. She was forced to leave on someone else's terms. There was nothing right about that, and nothing I could say to my parents to make it right. There's an old maxim that no parents should ever outlive their children. Those moments, with my mom in the dining room and my dad in the bathroom, were the reasons why. Our emotions make us who we are. They are the soul of each of us. And I can't think of anything that cuts deeper into one's soul than the harsh reality of finding out that your child has been taken from you forever.

While I was with Dad, Denise called Mini, who worked in equities at a local brokerage firm and was already at work since the stock market opens at 6:30 A.M. on the west coast.

"She's gone Mini. He did it. He finally killed her," is what Denise later told me she said. Mini was so stunned that she didn't show any emotion, neither at work nor on her drive home. She said it wasn't until she walked into the house and saw the misery in all of us that the reality of the situation hit her.

Our family spent the next several hours huddled closely around the dining room table consoling one another. We didn't talk about the specifics of what happened – I don't even know who knew what details at that point – but more the basic fact that our Nic, our Coco, was gone. As soon as we would start to compose ourselves and force some smiles and laughs as we reminisced about her, someone else would come through the front door: a neighbor, a relative, a friend, or a phone call would come in, or a delivery of flowers would be made, and we would all commence hugging and crying again.

The only person really missing was O.J., who was evidently in Chicago on a business trip. His friend and a friend of our family, A.C. Cowlings, who was also a former NFL player, called us that morning soon after we'd heard the news. He brought Sydney and Justin to the house for us. Both of the children had been home sleeping during the crime, but fortunately did not wake up until police got there. They never saw anything. They stayed at the police station overnight until A.C. picked them up and brought them over to us.

As the morning dragged on, we received more information from authorities about what happened. It was information we needed to know but didn't want to know. Nicole, they said, had been viciously attacked with a knife outside the front door of her condominium on Bundy Drive in Brentwood, probably around 10 or 10:30 P.M., soon after she got back from the restaurant. Her friend, Ronald Goldman, a wonderful man who worked at Mezzaluna, had stopped by her condo to drop off something for her after work. He was also killed on her doorstep in the same manner. Some of the details we heard about Nicole and Ron's deaths were gruesome, like something you might see on a crime show.

My God, I remember thinking. *Who could do that to another human being? And who would do that to Nicole and Ron?* Nicole didn't have any enemies that I knew of. She and O.J. had a sometimes tumultuous relationship since their divorce two years earlier, but he would never do something like that. And I still didn't think about what Denise said – that "He" killed her. Denise was absolutely positive, from the moment she heard the news, that it was him. I didn't even consider that possibility and still didn't think to ask who she thought "He" was. It was just not where I was in the grieving process at that early stage, nor was it appropriate to talk about at the time, especially with the kids there.

Later that morning, some of us moved into the living room and turned on the television to see if there were any more details on the news that had not yet been shared with us. I think we all assumed we might see a brief story on one of the local stations, but as I flipped channels while sitting next to Mom on the couch, we were shocked to learn how widespread word of Nicole's death was. If Nicole hadn't been tied to a former pro football player, few people outside of our area would have known or cared. But because she was, the news was on every television station, including the national networks. We thought about going over to Nicole's condo to see the scene firsthand, but with all of the attention it was already receiving, and with Nicole's children safe in our home, we decided it was best to lay low for a while. The speculation about why the crime happened and who did it hadn't yet begun, at least on the channels we were watching. But the story was obviously gaining momentum and was about to become one of the most notorious murder stories of the twentieth century.

I gripped Mom's hand as she stared stoically at the TV. We were seeing and hearing the same reports over and over, such as who was killed, where it happened, and when it happened, but with no real new facts until one station showed a video of a covered body.

It was Nicole's.

Draped in a white sheet, she was being loaded into the back of a van, like cargo, to be taken to the morgue. There were several gasps and not a dry eye in the room as we watched, mystified at what was taking place. We saw our cousin, Rolf, to whom we were so close that we called him our brother, standing near the body and talking to a police officer. I later asked him what they were talking about. He said he wanted to identify the body to spare us having to do so later, but the officer wouldn't let him or anyone else do it because of the brutality inflicted upon Nicole.

"We have a positive ID," he said the officer told him. "There is no reason for you or anybody else to see her in this condition."

Witnessing that on television was when it first became truly real for many of us. Being told over the phone that your sister or daughter is dead still leaves a slight glimmer of hope that maybe somebody made a mistake. Maybe somebody communicated something incorrectly. But actually seeing the body at Nicole's home as a reporter described what we were seeing – that was the finality of it.

That was when I could feel the hope drain from Mom as her hand trembled in mine.

"That's my kid," she softly cried as the back doors of the van were slammed shut. "That's my kid."

CHAPTER 8

THE VANILLA SCENT WAS GONE

*"For some reason, Nicole is coming to me a lot lately in
my dreams. I don't know why, but I have been thinking about
the crime scene. The coagulated blood. How Rolf cleaned it
up. No one cleaned it up before we got there."*

— November 4, 2004

The next day, early on Tuesday morning, we received a
phone call from authorities telling us that we could go into Nicole's condo and start packing up her belongings. I don't think
they had planned to necessarily let us in so soon, but they said
someone had thrown a rock from the street through a window,
and they expected it was only a matter of time before people
attempted to loot the place.

Dad, Mini, and I decided to go, and Rolf met us there.
Mom and Denise, meanwhile, went to the cemetery to pick out
a headstone. I would have preferred to go to the cemetery, but
going to the condo was something I felt I needed to do – to be
there for Dad and to try to help me better understand and cope
with what happened. Closure, maybe? No, but I felt I had to go
there and at least attempt to find it. I needed to see everything
for myself and not just rely on what the police and media were
showing or saying to us. I needed to try to say good-bye to my
sister. Was such a thing even possible two days later?

We drove to the condo, taking the route we usually took to
get there, but then veered off to some back roads as we got closer. We ultimately drove down an alley to the back of her home.

71

Police had told us they would be blocking off that general area so we could get through without any media or curious onlookers bothering us. We were told there may be throngs of people by the front gate on Bundy Drive, a main road in Brentwood.

We still didn't fully understand the public's obsession with Nicole's death, but it was something we wanted to avoid if possible. We parked in Nicole's driveway off the alley and entered through the door in the garage. That ended up being the only thing that went as we had planned. We soon found out that no matter how hard we tried to find peace with her death, the pain was going to be inescapable, lingering around every corner.

I followed Dad, Mini, and Rolf through the garage and into the condo. The second I stepped foot inside, I instantly felt that same choked-up sensation I had the previous day in the bathroom when Dad confirmed for me that Nicole was dead. Never did I expect to stumble upon such a scene.

Just moments after we got there, I learned it wasn't possible to try to say good-bye. In fact, it ended up being one of the most incredibly terrifying experiences of my life. Instead of finding closure, it inflicted fresh wounds into my already fragile mind.

> *"I saw a Ben & Jerry's melted ice cream cup at the bottom of the stairs, and the entire house was black with dust they used looking for fingerprints. I then saw her candles lit, the TV on, the radio on, and a knife on the kitchen counter. All I could picture was Nicole cooking eggs just a few weeks before for Sydney's First Communion party. And that radio - Nic always played music so loud. She would say 'Then turn it down if it's too loud.' She certainly wasn't going to do it. I remember seeing her jean jacket. There was lip gloss and gum in it. I took that and left the jacket. I don't know why. I just needed something from her. And this whole time there were investigators all over the house. We had no privacy at all."*
>
> *– November 4, 2004*

Nicole had taken the kids to Ben & Jerry's after dinner. It was just a small cup of ice cream she left behind, but it hit me hard because it represented so much about her: the fun mom that she was who took the time to take her kids out for a treat after an already long evening; the general happiness I always saw in her and the kids; the fact that it was the last thing she and her kids ever did together. There was even symbolism in the fact that something so good was left unfinished, melted into nothing, just like her life, and not by her choice.

And that knife on the counter – why was it out? It looked clean, like it hadn't been used for anything. Did she know the killer was out there? Did she get it out thinking she might need it to defend herself? Maybe she was just going to cut up some food. Was there any correlation at all between the ice cream, the knife, and her death? A million questions raced through my mind, and I had been in the condo for barely two minutes.

Then there were those walls. The once-pristine white walls throughout the home were now an eerie, dirty black, all covered with fingerprint dust. It made the place look dark and creepy, like a scene from an old haunted house movie. A heavy aura of fear lingered throughout. That fresh vanilla scent it always used to have, Nicole's favorite fragrance, was gone. It didn't look or feel anything like her home that I had visited so many times before, where she was raising her two beautiful children, where she was living her new life after the divorce. It was now just a cold, lifeless, abandoned building, the essence of it destroyed.

With our eyes welling up, we continued to cautiously step through, nervous about what we might find in the next room or behind the next door. Rolf went ahead on his own, I think to see what he could find to either hide from us or to warn us about to lessen the shock. Dad and Mini held up pretty well. Dad was being strong like he felt a dad should. Mini was being Mini – a doer, keeping her emotions in check with a mission of getting things packed up and moved out.

But I couldn't take it. I became so overwhelmed by the sickening sight of what Nicole's home had become and the thought of how she died, that my stomach twisted into knots. I felt like I was going to throw up. With investigators seemingly all around us in every room we entered, I wanted to find any privacy I could. I told my family I'd be right back and raced up the stairs to the bathroom off of Nicole's bedroom. But the scene was just as nauseating when I walked in there.

"Oh God!" I shrieked, covering my mouth in shock.

It looked like Nicole had just been there. The candles she kept all around her bathtub were lit. The tub was full of water, an obvious sign that she was about to take a bath before going to bed that night. All that was missing was Nicole. I think all five stages of grief rattled through my brain in the few seconds I was there. I assume everything was as it was because investigators didn't want to alter anything until they had all of the evidence they needed – just like the ice cream and the knife downstairs. But it absolutely scared the hell out of me, instantaneously filling my mind with irrational fears. What if the killer did this to scare us? What if he were still hiding somewhere inside? Was he watching me? What if I were next? I looked up at the skylight and realized he could come crashing through it and attack me. I was so terrified and numb that I couldn't even throw up. I dashed out of the room more quickly than I had entered it, scampered through the hall, and charged down the steps to be with my dad and sister. I tried to look composed, though I know I failed.

"You okay?" Mini asked.

"Yeah, I'm fine," I lied, my voice shaking, not about to tell them what I found.

We continued to gingerly make our way through the main floor of the condo, not searching for anything in particular. Just looking. Remembering. Wishing things were back to the way they once were. And yes, maybe wondering if we might find a clue investigators missed as to what happened, or who did it, or why. I knew that was unrealistic, but a lot of irrational thoughts run through your mind when you're in a situation like that.

After going through most of the rooms, we finally reached the front door. Though we never talked about it, I think we all tried to avoid it as long as we could, knowing that on the other side of that door was where Nicole and Ron's bodies were found. But there was nowhere else for us to go. The time had come to open it. I guess we had the option of not opening it, but I think we all felt like we had to. We had to confront what happened. We had to see it for ourselves. We knew her body wouldn't be there, but there was a part of me that feared she might be, especially after seeing what I'd just seen in the bathroom.

There is nothing there, I kept telling myself. *Nothing there. They took her away yesterday. It's over. She's gone.*

I took a deep breath as Daddy slowly pulled the door open. The first thing I recall is hearing a noise, like rushing water. Being so dark inside, it took my eyes a few seconds to adjust to the bright sunlight. Once they did ...

"Ahhhh!" I screeched, drawing both of my hands over my mouth and nose.

Rolf was standing there with a garden hose, washing away what was obviously blood, hoping that he'd get it all cleaned before we got out there. I guess it wasn't the responsibility of the investigators to clean it up, but I never in a million years expected it to be left there like that. I started to feel sick again. But just like I kept it down when I was distracted in the bathroom, the same thing happened to me outside. The distraction this time, though, was all the noise on the other side of the front gate caused by the people the police had protected us from when we'd arrived there. It was a mob of dozens, probably hundreds, crammed on Bundy Drive, and it was complete pandemonium.

Media trucks topped with satellite dishes were parked for as far as we could see. Some reporters were doing live reports, while others were just hanging out searching for whatever bit of sensational minutiae they could find. The rest were everyday people who wanted to get a glimpse of what I didn't realize was becoming a huge part of history. They waved and shouted at us. I have no idea what they said; there were so many of them yelling. It was as if the gate was a prison cell and they were the prisoners, making all kinds of racket and wanting to bust the door down and charge through. There was also a lot of noise from helicopters hovering overhead. What were they doing up there? What did they expect to see from up there? I soon realized *we* were the prisoners.

Daddy turned to Mini and me, his face grim.

"Go back inside," he calmly said to us. "Rolf and I will take care of things out here."

I came to the realization when we finally left the condo that the public fascination with my sister's death was all about O.J. as the rumors floating out there that he was the killer were heating up.

While the average person who followed the case back then might say "Of course he was a suspect," it wasn't that simple for me. I'd known him for nearly twenty years, since I was seven years old. Growing up, he wasn't a star football player to me. He wasn't a celebrity. He was my sister's husband. My brother-in-law. My family. My friend. In fact, given the age difference between us, I usually referred to him as Uncle O.J. when I was little, someone I looked up to who always treated me well. Even after the divorce, I still considered him family because he was the father of my niece and nephew.

The next few days would be about as surreal as they could get, and probably a little more surreal to me than to most people. While many people within and outside of my family believed that O.J. certainly could have been, or was, responsible for murdering Nicole, I really struggled to accept that he could have had anything to do with it.

CHAPTER 9

THE EPITOME OF DOMESTIC VIOLENCE

"Nicole was a very strong-willed human being. Anyone of this sort will hide a lot because of embarrassment or pride. Those out there who have been victims of domestic violence will understand this. Those who have not may never understand."

— October 27, 2004

The first time I met O.J. was when Nicole brought him to our house after they met at a restaurant where she was waitressing. It was around 1977. He was thirty, she was just eighteen. Yes, a huge age difference, but that didn't seem to matter to her or anyone in the family. He was still playing for the Buffalo Bills that year, but he had a home in Southern California where he had gone to college at USC. When Nicole brought him over that first time, he sat at our dining room table with all of us Brown women, none of us knowing or caring a lick about football. To us, he wasn't a celebrity. He was just a guy, Nicole's boyfriend, and that was it. He was very amicable, had a wonderful presence about him, and wore an infectious smile. Nicole and he eventually married in 1985, and I loved him as much as any other person in our family.

Sure, as a kid, some of my love for him may have stemmed from the things he and Nicole bought me. They surprised me with my first Barbie dollhouse and my first ten-speed bike. When he played for the San Francisco 49ers in 1979, Nicole drove me up there to see him play, which included stops on the way at Disneyland, Knott's Berry Farm, and Hearst Castle, a dream trip for any kid my age. But my love for him went beyond the material things. We had great times together as a family, which always seemed to mean just as much to him.

I recall one Thanksgiving at his and Nicole's home on Rockingham Avenue in Brentwood when he came up behind me and whispered out of the blue: "I'm so thankful for your family because they are so much my family." It was a beautiful thing to say, but not out of the ordinary for him, at least from my perspective. That's just the kind of guy he seemed to be. Another time, when I was fourteen years old and at a church youth group meeting making crosses out of palms, we were instructed to give them to someone we loved, but to whom we'd never said "I love you." I gave mine to O.J.

He even reached out to me emotionally and financially just six months prior to Nicole's death in a way only a family member or great friend would. It was a few days after Christmas in 1993, around that time I mentioned earlier – when I was having difficulty at UC San Diego and was considering dropping out. I was home for break and was hanging out with Nicole and O.J. at their beach house in Laguna Beach (yes, they were divorced at the time, but he was still always treated as part of our family because of Sydney and Justin. Nicole never shut him out of their lives). We were talking again about my situation in school. Not only was I struggling academically, but I was also having a hard time paying my tuition each semester. I wasn't asking them for help but was just blowing off some steam. In fact, I had made up my mind that I was going to throw in the towel there and go to school somewhere closer to home come January. But O.J. wouldn't let me.

"I'd hate to see you give up on something you really want," he said to me. "Try one more semester and I'll pay for it."

"But money isn't the main problem," I said. "I'm just not getting the grades, even though I'm really trying."

"I understand," he replied. "But if you let me pay for the next semester, that will at least temporarily eliminate the financial stress so you can focus solely on your school work."

I gave him a hug and agreed to take him up on his offer. What did I have to lose? And it felt great that he and Nicole cared that much to try to help me. But the results didn't change. In May 1994, at the end of the semester, my grades weren't any better, my stress level wasn't any lower, and I decided it was time to transfer out. My first weekend home after school ended was Mother's Day, and the whole family was in the courtyard celebrating. After Mom opened her gifts, I asked O.J. if we could go inside and talk in private. We went back to my room and I gave him a check for the amount of money he spent on my tuition that semester. I felt it was the honorable thing to do after all he had done for me. He gave me a big hug.

"At least you tried," he said. "I'm proud of you for that."

That was the brother-in-law I always knew.

But less than one month after giving him that check, after Nicole was found dead, I was shocked to learn about the brother-in-law I didn't know, a man most people didn't know – a mean, hateful, sinister, evil man who brutalized my sister with verbal and physical beat downs for years and years. It was the epitome of domestic violence cases, from the way he treated her to the way she reacted to it.

Denise knew something about it when she saw bruises on Nicole one day years earlier, and Nicole told her they were from O.J. Nicole even had Denise take photos to document it. But when Denise later asked Nicole what she was doing about it, Nicole told her to forget it, that everything was fine. Despite Denise's concerns and persistent questions, Nicole insisted it was no longer an issue and demanded that she drop it. Nicole, like many victims of domestic violence, was very good at hiding the violence from everybody, even those closest to her, or shrugging it off and claiming it was no big deal. With Denise having no experience with domestic violence issues and receiving no cooperation from Nicole, all she could do was believe and trust her sister that everything was okay.

In another incident, in 1989, O.J. was arrested for attacking Nicole at their home after a New Year's Eve party, an episode that became public because of a 911 call Nicole made that night. My parents didn't tell me about it because they didn't want to upset me, and I didn't hear anything about it on my own until he went to court, where he was basically let off the hook, given a small fine and no jail time. Again, it was an occurrence later downplayed by Nicole, at least to us. Should we have known it could develop one day into a life and death issue? Reflecting on it years later, of course. But we, too, were uneducated on the subject of domestic violence. After the abuse that night, and after he walked out of court with nothing more than a slightly thinner wallet, Nicole went on with her life as if nothing had happened.

But the second Denise found out Nicole had been killed, she knew O.J. did it. She had no direct proof. She did not know yet about the many damning pieces of evidence against him, such as his blood in his car, the bloody glove found outside his house, the witnesses who would testify, and the extensive photos beyond what she took that one day of Nicole that showed the bruises and cuts he inflicted upon her. But Denise just knew from what little Nicole told her about the abuse and from a sister's and best friend's intuition, that it had to be him.

Those revelations about him and the way he dehumanized Nicole left me beyond perplexed in the days immediately following her death. I did not want to believe he did it and fought that notion in my mind as much as I could, but the evidence and public opinion were mounting. How could he have done it, though? How could I have known this guy since I was seven years old and not known that side of him, that he was capable of doing something as barbarous as this?

On that Tuesday afternoon, after we packed up some things at the condo and after Denise and Mom picked out the headstone, Denise met Dad, Mini, and me at O'Connor Mortuary to arrange the details of Nicole's viewing and funeral. The owner's son, Neil, who was an employee there and also a friend of mine since childhood, asked me how I was doing.

"Well, that &*#%*$ killed my sister," I said nonchalantly about my former brother-in-law, without any doubt in my voice. Wow! Where did that come from? It was the first time I said he did it after telling myself over and over that he didn't do it. That revealing opinion, however, was short-lived as I turned 180 degrees on Wednesday night at the viewing when I walked up to O.J. and gave him a hug.

"We're going to get through this," I whispered in his ear. He nodded and gave me a faint smile.

Confused? Imagine how I felt. I just told the "&*#%*$" who I claimed killed my sister that we were going to get through this? I don't think I knew what was real and what wasn't. Every event that extended from her death, such as going through her home, seeing her dead body at the mortuary, hearing rumors about O.J., seeing him for myself – it all had me so discombobulated.

On Thursday, at Nicole's funeral, the pendulum swung back the other way as my doubts about him surfaced again. I rode in the limousine with him and the kids from the funeral at the church to the cemetery for Nicole's burial. Everybody was quiet, pretty much in a stupor after such a mentally draining service, staring at the floor or out the windows. Me? I was staring at the cut on his finger for the first time. It was a deep cut that all the media had been talking about that week. He said it was from a broken glass when he was in his Chicago hotel room, but skeptics claimed it was the result of his physical struggles with Nicole and Ron.

There it is, I thought to myself in the limo. *There's the cut. I guess a piece of glass could have caused that. Or maybe not. Maybe he did kill her. But he was in Chicago so soon after she was killed. Could he have really gone to his daughter's dance recital, committed such a heinous crime a couple hours later, then gotten on a plane and left town as if nothing happened? Is this all an act right now? Is he attending the funeral of the woman he murdered?*

But instead of emotionally shifting back the other way, as had been my norm, my doubts were compounded the next day when he captivated a reported ninety-five million TV viewers nationwide, including my family, with his infamous low-speed highway chase. Yes, ninety-five million, an estimated five million more viewers than had watched the Super Bowl earlier that year. He was supposed to turn himself in to police that Friday morning to face double murder charges, but instead he rode in the back seat of his white Bronco driven by A.C. Cowlings, threatening to kill himself with a gun he held to his head. Most people who remember that may recall later hearing the recording of Detective Lange trying to talk O.J. into surrendering during the chase. But what many people don't know is that Denise and my dad also tried to talk him down. They were at the condo with Mini, packing more stuff, when O.J. called there. He evidently assumed somebody in the family would be there, and he guessed correctly. No matter what Dad and Denise's personal feelings were toward him at the time, they were thinking solely about Sydney and Justin, who had just lost their mother. They didn't need to lose their father, too.

"Don't do it, Juice!" Daddy urged him, calling him by his well-known nickname and trying to get him to put the gun down and pull over. "Think of your two kids, Juice! Don't do it!"

That was one of the most surreal of the countless bizarre moments for me during this saga. A day after riding in the limo with O.J. to bury my sister, here I was watching dozens of officers with the California Highway Patrol on national television slowly chasing him. My dad was on the phone trying to stop him. Denise and Dominique, meanwhile, had jumped in the car and were on their way to the cemetery to try to stop him from killing himself at Nicole's grave, in case that's where he was headed. *Are you kidding me?* I thought to myself as all of this chaos was unfolding. Some of the most creative writers in the world couldn't have developed a drama like this. And this was *my* family this was happening to! Everything had been so normal in our lives just one week earlier. What happened? How? Why?

O.J. eventually surrendered that night at his Rockingham home, pleaded not guilty in court, and went to jail until the trial proceedings began a few months later. But I didn't need to wait that long for my doubts about him to be solidified. Just a couple days after all of the Bronco-chase hype, the phone rang in my bedroom. It was my own private line, so I knew the call was intended specifically for me, and I was shocked to hear who was on the other end.

It was O.J. He was calling from jail.

"Hey, Tanya, it's Juice," he said with some pep in his voice. He didn't stop talking long enough to let me say hi or ask why he was calling me. He went right into what sounded like a defense he was trying to build for himself for his criminal trial, as if I were the judge and jury.

"Hey, you know I loved your sister, right?"

"Uhhh ... I really don't know," I said, totally uncomfortable with the question.

"C'mon, Tanya, I would have taken a bullet for her."

"Okaaaay," I said, unsure of what he expected me to say. I didn't like the tone or direction of the conversation at all, so I tried to change the subject. It was a morbid subject but with more relevance. At least *I* thought so. I told him that a man he knew very well, the father of a friend of mine, recently had an aneurism and was near death.

"It doesn't look like he's going to make it," I said, fighting back tears.

"What?" he said with astonishment. No, not astonishment that a man I thought he cared about was about to die, but that I would have the nerve to focus on anyone but O.J. Simpson. "Why are you worried about that? What about me?" he said. "I'm stuck here in this tiny cell." I was so stunned that I couldn't reply. He continued to babble about his woes and actually tried to put the entire blame on Nicole for their marriage falling apart. He talked about how he and his current girlfriend would lay in bed each morning and read the newspaper while talking about politics and current events.

This is so surreal, I thought. *Where is he going with this?*

"What did your sister ever do?" he asked me, as if his relationship with his girlfriend was on some higher intellectual level than the one he had with Nicole, and that Nicole was to blame for that. And he was throwing this at me just a week after her death and just a few days after we said our final goodbyes to her.

I was incensed, seething, enraged.

"What did she do?" I shouted. "She dedicated her life to you – to your career! She gave you two beautiful children! She was a homemaker for your family! She ..."

Click.

"Hello? Hello? Are you listening to me? Hello?"

He was gone. I don't know if the time allotted for his call was up, or if he hung up on me, but the conversation ended abruptly. I slammed the phone down and I cried.

I just cried.

It was at that moment that I knew I could no longer deny the suspicions that so many others had. It was at that moment that I knew what he had done to my sister.

CHAPTER 10

THE LITTLE VOICE

"I just went on and on hysterically today about Nicole. The rage, anger, and sadness I have about Nicole and how I never coped with it. We never talked about it as a family or with a therapist. We just kind of didn't talk about it. Out of respect for the family and kids, we just didn't talk about it. Now after 10 years I'm talking about how much it angers me that she never took advantage of the many times she had with me to discuss her fear of OJ. Not once. I also got mad at myself for not seeing the dangers when I helped her move from Rockingham."

— November 11, 2004

On that Tuesday when we packed some of Nicole's things at her condo just before meeting Denise at the mortuary, we opened any drawers, boxes, and envelopes we found to make sure we weren't missing anything that might be immediately important to have. As we were going through the drawers in her nightstand, we discovered a key for a safe deposit box at a local bank. Not giving much thought to what might be in it other than probably some jewelry or other personal valuables, law enforcement authorities went ahead and checked it out. When they did, we were astonished to find that it contained documentation, including photos Nicole had taken, of the physical abuse O.J. inflicted upon her. Three days later, when Denise, Mini, and Dad were back at the condo, Mini found a random cardboard box in a kitchen cupboard with diaries

85

Nicole kept, more evidence of the abuse and pain Nicole endured.

"You're a fat pig ... you're disgusting ... you're a slob ... I want you out of my &*#%*$@ house!" she penned him as saying in one of his many tirades toward her, also noting in her writing that she was two months pregnant at the time. *"He proceeded to cut me down. I tried to tape the conversation, but the recorder didn't work,"* she wrote.

And thus began my education into the inauspicious world of domestic violence.

The National Coalition Against Domestic Violence defines domestic violence as thoroughly and pointedly as anything can be defined:

The willful intimidation, physical assault, battery, sexual assault, and/or other abusive behavior perpetrated by an intimate partner against another. It is an epidemic affecting individuals in every community, regardless of age, economic status, race, religion, nationality or educational background. Violence against women is often accompanied by emotionally abusive and controlling behavior, and thus is part of a systematic pattern of dominance and control. Domestic violence results in physical injury, psychological trauma, and sometimes death. The consequences of domestic violence can cross generations and truly last a lifetime.

The links between domestic violence and mental illness are clear. Several studies have shown that women who experience violence from their intimate partners are often diagnosed with a psychiatric disorder, such as depression, anxiety, or post-traumatic stress. According to Suicide.org, twenty-five percent of women who experience domestic violence attempt suicide.

I never heard Nicole talk about depression, but then again, I didn't talk about it either while I was going through it. There is no doubt in my mind that she silently suffered from it for a long time during her abusive relationship. She had to. She even implemented the coping tool of journaling, which is how we learned about the abuse with which she was living.

"He beat me up so bad at home – tore my blue sweater and blue slacks completely off me," Nicole wrote in another one of her diaries. *"I went to the hospital and claimed it to be a bicycle accident."*

According to a Senate Judiciary Committee report, domestic violence is the leading cause of injury to women between the ages of fifteen and forty-four in the U.S., more than muggings, rapes, and car accidents combined. If more people were educated on domestic violence and batterer treatment programs, maybe the frequency of domestic violence would diminish, along with the number of cases of depression. I can only imagine what Nicole and I might have been able to do for each other, the support we could have given each other, if we had both spoken up.

Those dangers about which I journaled at the beginning of this chapter, the dangers that I was mad at myself for not seeing, included three instances in 1992. They were all at about the time Nicole divorced O.J., but they did not become evident to me until after her death.

The first two were almost identical situations: both at their Rockingham house, both on the same day, and both involving me helping Nicole pack her stuff so she and the kids could move out of there. In the first instance, I was in her bedroom with the door open when we heard O.J. come in through the front door.

"Close the door and lock it!" she said in a harsh whisper.

"What?" I said, wondering why on earth she wanted us to be locked in the bedroom, and why she would want him locked out.

"Just close it and lock it now!" she demanded.

I did – and saw a look of panic on her face.

"Are you okay?" I asked.

"Get Daddy on the phone," she said. "And don't talk … the phones might be tapped!"

What the hell is going on? I thought. *Phones tapped?* I called Dad as she asked, but obviously I had to talk once he answered. I told him what was happening and he seemed as confused as I was, but he told me to stay on the line and let him know what was going on. O.J. knocked on the door.

"Nicole?" he shouted.

"Not now!" she shot back. "We're busy packing."

"He is knocking on the bedroom door, but Nicole told him to go away because we're packing," I told Dad.

"What's he doing now?" Dad asked a few seconds later.

"Nothing, I guess. I don't hear anything. I think he left," I replied.

And that was it. He did, in fact, walk away. I told Daddy everything seemed fine and we hung up.

Wow, was that weird. What has gotten into her? Why was she so rude to him? I wondered, thinking this must just be something that happens when two people divorce. Looking back on it, I was foolish to not read more into her actions, but I didn't know any better. I'd known my brother-in-law for fifteen years. He was family. Never did I consider interpreting her fear as a sign that there was something wrong beyond the fact that he was the man she was divorcing.

The second instance was just a couple hours later. Again, I was helping her pack, this time in Sydney's room, when O.J. came to that bedroom door. I was looking at Nicole with my back to him. I could tell by her look that something was wrong. I turned around and saw him standing there.

"Oh, hey," I said.

"Hi Tanya," he replied with a smile.

"Don't talk to him!" Nicole said tersely. "C'mon, let's get this stuff packed." He just shook his head without saying anything, shrugged his shoulders at me as if to say "Oh well," and walked away.

Sheeesh! I thought. *What is her problem? Just because they're splitting up means I can't say hi? And why did she have to be so mean to him again?*

I don't know if it was because she was so angry or because I was in her house, but I didn't feel comfortable asking her any questions about it at the time. As far as I knew, their divorce was over the standard "irreconcilable differences," which to me meant they simply weren't getting along and were not in love with each other anymore. So as long as they weren't fighting in front of me, I felt the best thing to do was let it all go.

The third time was the most bizarre. It was many weeks later, the divorce had officially gone through, and she was living at her new place. My girlfriend and I were visiting her there when Nicole asked if we'd go over to Rockingham and pick up the minivan. Sure, no problem. O.J. was there when we arrived, so my friend and I sat in a little TV area off the kitchen, chatting with him for about fifteen minutes. When we got back to Nicole's, I was expecting a "thank you." Instead, she absolutely ripped into me.

"Where the hell have you been?" she screamed.

"What? What do you mean where have I been? We got your van."

"Why did it take you so long?"

"I don't know," I said. "We stayed and talked for a few minutes, but that's it." I didn't get it. Was she worried that I stopped off somewhere with her van?

"Next time I ask you to get the van, just get the van!" she exclaimed.

I didn't know what to say. My girlfriend was stunned. Nicole had turned to walk away, but this time I couldn't let it go.

"Hey, what's your problem?" I said.

She spun around with a look of rage I'd never seen from her.

"What's my problem?" she fired back, marching toward me and not stopping until she was right in my face. "I asked you to get my van and that's it! How hard is it to do that?"

I shut my mouth, stepped back, put my hands up to signal that I'd surrendered, and our discussion was over. Knowing now the mental and physical torture she went through with him, she had every right to be angry with me. But I didn't know. The signs were there. They were there for years. But I was totally ignorant about domestic violence and her situation.

Since Nicole's death, our family has learned and publicly spoken about domestic violence issues, trying to help women, men, and children understand the warning signs and what to do when it's happening. Denise has spoken extensively about it across the nation and has testified in Washington, D.C., before Congress, advocating for stiffer laws. I have also made domestic violence a part of my talks because of its ties to depression, including the stigma that comes with both. People are afraid to admit that they are being abused. They are embarrassed to come forward. Some keep quiet because they are holding out false hope that today will be the day it finally ends.

But we cannot judge women who continue to return to these relationships. Statistics show a woman will go back multiple times before she actually leaves. Women love their mates. They endure the violence while continuing to wait for the man they married to return. They know the charmer that is hidden behind the evil. Nicole said to my mom once, "He will always be my soul mate." That right there shows how they think. But when a victim does come forward, that cycle of violence breaks – for that person and for future generations in that family. That's why it is so important for victims to courageously seek help and for others to take note of warning signs that someone may be a victim. Then step up and help.

The late, great actor Christopher Reeve once said, "I think we all have a little voice inside us that will guide us. It may be God, I don't know. But I think that if we shut out all the noise and clutter from our lives and listen to the voice, it will tell us the right thing to do."

How true for those who suffer with depression or are victims of violence. How true for those of us who suspect people we know and love are going through either of those circumstances. How true for all of us in any situation. We need that voice – or someone's voice – to intervene, and we have to listen to it. We simply cannot go it alone.

I only wish I had known that fact when my depression first kicked in after Herissa's death, or at least soon after Nicole's death. It might have helped me get through the trial, keep my job, and come to terms more easily with the world's fascination over the hell my family was going through.

CHAPTER 11

WHEN SOMEBODY DOES AN O.J. ON YOU

"Suddenly, I felt cameras on me, and I hated it. This was not a game to me. This was not a circus. This should not have been about who was going to get the highest ratings. My sister had been brutally murdered, and she was not here to defend herself. We had to do it."

— October 28, 2004

From the murders in June 1994 to the verdict in the criminal trial in October 1995, nothing in the world received more media attention. Nothing. No other tragedies. No other deaths. Not even wars around the world. It seemed like the *Los Angeles Times* had at least one story about the trial on its front page almost every day during that time. The nightly network newscasts dedicated far more attention to the trial than to other events that should have been considered much more newsworthy, in my opinion.

I have talked to people who said they would rush home from work and flip on their televisions just to see what happened in the case that day – and some who would follow it at work, likely resulting in lost productivity at many businesses. In the eyes of the general public, each day seemed to bring something new, fascinating, and sometimes downright ridiculous about witnesses, jurors, or evidence. It was reality television before reality television existed as we know it today, and people of all ages from every corner of the globe could not get enough of it.

While that was available daily for public consumption, there was the other behind-the-scenes reality show going on that most people weren't privy to: the perpetual scrutiny my family had to endure. It was beyond what even the brightest Hollywood minds could have ever conceived.

Helicopters flew over our house so low and so often that when I hear one above us today, it's still my first instinct to think it is there to videotape us. The day after Nicole's funeral, on that Friday when Denise, Mini, and Dad were inside Nicole's condo and the Bronco chase was about to begin, helicopters from local television stations suddenly swooped in from nowhere over the condo "like it was Armageddon," Denise later told me. The media was evidently tipped off that our family was there. I have no idea why they cared so much or what kind of video they thought they'd get, but they hunted my sisters and Dad down and swarmed around them with all of the reinforcements they had.

And it didn't stop there.

During the trial, any time Mom had to take Sydney and Justin somewhere, she would walk them from the front door of our house to the car in the driveway with coats or blankets over their heads to shield them from the helicopters' cameras. You probably thought Michael Jackson was the one who started that with his kids. Sydney and Justin thought it was funny, like it was a game of hide-n-seek. Mom – well, like everything else, she rolled with it, but she didn't see much humor in the personal lives of her innocent grandchildren being invaded.

TV trucks with enormous satellite dishes and boom microphones camped on the main highway behind our home, congesting the street and annoying our neighbors. Who could blame them? We were more annoyed than they were. If we pulled out of the neighborhood, camera crews chased us every step they could just to get a shot of us leaving. When we had conversations in our home, we brought our voices down to near whispers because we were afraid those gigantic microphones aimed toward us would pick up what we were saying.

One Saturday, when much of the media had dispersed for the weekend, we were able to sneak out for a short walk along the beach. It was like a band of prisoners being allowed to experience fresh air without their cuffs or shackles. But when we got back to the house, a newspaper reporter was there. No, not outside our front door, but sitting on our couch. Yes, in our house, waiting for us. He got in simply by walking in. Our neighborhood, a gated community, had always been a very safe place with virtually no crime. But this guy found a way to sneak in from the beach. Locking our doors had never been necessary. We now realized that was unfortunately going to have to change.

We received death threats on a routine basis from people who thought O.J. was innocent. I assumed most of them were crank calls, but how could we know for sure? We didn't. Based on the way people behaved during the Bronco chase and outside Nicole's condominium when we were there the week after she died, yelling and cheering and treating the situation like it was a game, we couldn't put anything past anyone.

Don't get me wrong – there were also many people who provided us with a ton of support during the whole ordeal. Hundreds of them. In fact, many of them were strangers, sending us gifts and love from around the world. The level of comfort from people who understood our plight was truly amazing, and we will forever be grateful for their love and kindness. But based on sheer numbers, the gawking and assault on our privacy every moment of every day – especially the incomprehensible threats people made on our lives – often overshadowed the good things many people did for us.

This went on nonstop, around the clock, throughout the nearly eighteen months of the legal process. Looking back on it now, I sort of understand the level of fascination the media and public had with it. It was a case that involved a Hall of Fame football player, a guy many knew not just from his exploits on the field, but from his warm smile and friendly demeanor that came across in those humorous Hertz car rental commercials he did back in the 1970s. O.J. Simpson was pretty much a household name, and the thought that he could kill two people, and in such a brutal way, was unfathomable to a nation that treats its athletes like heroes. But for it to be taken to the level that it was, as if it were the most important news on the planet, is still baffling to me.

I have little doubt that if I had gone outside my house at any point and told reporters that I just ate a sandwich, I could have turned around, gone back into the house, and seen it immediately reported on TV as breaking news with "experts" weighing in on what kind of sandwich I ate and how it related to the case. I cannot stress enough how taxing it was on my family.

Specifically for me, not having the mental strength that the rest of my family had, it was a very traumatic and unhealthy stretch of my life as I felt psychologically debilitated almost on a daily basis. The very last thing someone going through depression wants is unsolicited attention. She wants to be left alone. She doesn't want people peppering her with questions. She doesn't want intrusive noises. She certainly doesn't want cameras on her. She doesn't want anyone or anything disrupting her life in any way. Any of that can create a pressure that sends her mind into overload, leaving her feeling overwhelmed, confused, and angry, rendering her virtually hopeless in every aspect of her life.

I was working for a structural engineering firm during the trial, doing a lot of administrative work that included handling client files. I tried to attend as many of the court dates as I could because I felt I needed to be there for Nicole and our family, but attending every day was not possible due to my job. I was twenty-four or twenty-five years old at the time. I had to find a way to balance supporting Nicole, my family, and my own desire to be in court while still earning a living. But I never could find that equilibrium.

While I may have handled the actual number of days I was at work versus the number of days I was in court fairly well, I was out of whack mentally. Whether going to court or work, I struggled to get out of bed in the mornings. I felt like whichever one I chose, I was in a no-win situation. Do I go listen to more gory details about my sister's death while a family member targeted as the alleged killer sits a few feet away from me, or do I go to work and worry all day about what was transpir-

ing in court that I was missing? This was my life. When I went
to bed at night, I felt so weighed down that I would often cry
myself to sleep. I became an ineffective person all around.

After giving me many opportunities to get my act together,
the company had to finally let me go. I was screwing up too
much – messing up files, filing things in the wrong places, forcing my coworkers and superiors to lose confidence in me. I
was becoming a liability to them. I couldn't argue with their
decision for two reasons: one was that I truly was messing up,
and the other was that I did not want my identity revealed. Of
course people knew that I was Tanya Brown, but only a handful knew that I was Nicole Brown Simpson's sister. I asked our
human resources department to help me keep it quiet from
everyone so that it wouldn't cause any more distractions for
me, and I appreciated that they cooperated. Work was the one
place where I could be sure I would get some peace from the
chaos of the trial, and where I could be safe from "moles" tip-
ping off the media about every trivial thing I was doing. I did
not want to change that, even if it ended up costing me my job.

That peace – mental, physical, emotional, spiritual – is ultimately what someone with depression seeks. It is a peace
that eluded me during the trial, whether I was at home where
the media was practically living with us, or outside our home
where everybody talked nonstop about the case.

A perfect example was in the fall of 1994, three months after Nicole's death and just days prior to the selection of the
jury. I was sitting in a psychology class at California State University San Marcos where I had just transferred from UC San
Diego. My professor was lecturing about a relatively unknown
murder case and was talking in detail about how the victim
was killed with a knife. But instead of just leaving it at that, he
said with a laugh, "You know what I'm talking about. When
somebody does an O.J. on you."

Gulp!

I was floored. *Did he really just say that?* I did my best to stay
calm, even though I felt I had every right to rip into him right
then and there. But the professor didn't know my relationship
to Nicole, and the other students probably didn't either since I

was new on campus. There was no need to cause a scene and give them something more to talk about outside of class. I paid little attention to the rest of his lecture, instead contemplating during the remainder of class how to handle what he said.

Just let it go, Tanya, I kept telling myself over and over again. *He said it, it's done, just let it go. He doesn't know who you are. He wouldn't have said it if he did. Just forget it.*

But I couldn't. When class was over, I followed him to his office. I stayed poised and didn't raise any havoc, but I was very blunt.

"I just wanted to let you know something," I said. "You really need to be careful how you present things in your class because you never know who you are talking to."

"Okay," he said with a confused look on his face. "Can I ask what this is about?"

"Yes," I said. "I'm Nicole Brown Simpson's sister."

It took him a couple of seconds to realize why I would be sharing that with him, but once the light bulb went on, his face changed colors faster than a chameleon. He was very embarrassed, and he apologized profusely.

"Just be happy it was me in your class and not one of my sisters," I said. "They wouldn't have been so kind. I'm just too tired from all of this stuff to put up a fight."

I wasn't oblivious to the fact that people made comments like that, or that there were other jokes floating out there. They were all in poor taste from my perspective, of course, but I had to pick my battles and not try to fight every one. I don't think I was educated enough to know that was the healthy way to handle myself, as I would later learn at South Coast. It was more that I was just too mentally exhausted to be constantly fighting with people.

When I did pick battles, however, I went hard at my targets. As I stated earlier, there are different criteria for determining if someone suffers from depression. One word you can apply to all of the criteria, though, is "extreme." You may feel tired all the time or you may struggle to sleep – complete opposites, but whichever way you feel, it is to the extreme. You may move slowly or be very restless – either way, it's to an extreme. So if I weren't keeping extremely calm, like I did toward my professor after his comment, I was chewing out somebody. There rarely was any middle ground.

One example was the night of the viewing of Nicole's body. O.J. brought an entourage of people with him, including one of his attorneys. The investigation into the murder was well under way, which I guess is why the attorney felt he had to be there with his client. Unfortunately, he checked his manners at the door and decided to conduct business inside the mortuary. At the same time he was doing that, I had tried a couple of times to go into the room where Nicole's body was laid out, but it was just too emotionally difficult. I sat by myself crying on a couch in the lobby while the attorney was in a chair diagonal to my left. As I was sobbing, he totally ignored me, talking on his cell phone to somebody about something that had nothing to do with my sister's viewing. His voice may have been on an even keel, but in my mind it was getting louder and louder, and more and more irritating. I couldn't bite my tongue any longer.

"Hey!" I yelled at him.

He didn't even look up.

"Hey!" I yelled louder.

This time he looked up and appeared stunned.

"Hold ... hold on a second," he said into his phone. He pulled the phone from his ear and was about to say something, but I didn't give him the chance.

"How about showing a little respect for my sister and my family!" I screamed. Other people passing through the lobby stopped to watch, but I didn't care. "This isn't the place to be talking on the phone. We're in a mortuary. Take your call outside!"

He didn't apologize, but at least he listened and got up and walked away.

Another occasion I showed no room for compromise was when I went to visit Nicole's grave one afternoon soon after her death. It wasn't her birthday or any other special day. I was just in the mood to go sit by her and quietly talk to her.

*"As I approached her gravesite, there were two women,
two cameramen, and another woman with a notepad hovering over my sister. I initially didn't know what to do, but
figured I had two choices: I could leave and allow them not to
let my sister rest in peace as she deserved, or I could defend
her with everything I had. I chose option two."*

– October 28, 2004

I walked quickly toward them with my arms flailing, and
I didn't hold back.

"Are you serious?" I yelled. "Are you serious? Can't you
let her rest? Even at the cemetery, the one place on earth where
somebody should truly be able to rest?"

Both cameramen lifted up their cameras and brazenly
pointed them at me.

"Turn them off! Turn them off now!" I screamed, about
ready to get physical with them. "You know, if you were here
to pay your respects, that's one thing, but you're not!"

The woman with the notepad walked closer to me.

"I know how awful this has to be for you to see us here,"
she said. I looked at her with complete astonishment, then
clenched my teeth as hard as I could to try to help me stay
somewhat calm.

"You have absolutely no idea how awful this is," I said
slowly.

"Well, we're here to do a story, and ..."

"I don't care about your story, I don't care who you are,
and I don't care who you are with!" I cried.

"Do you mind if I ask you your name?"

Arrgh! I was so blown away by her nerve to ask that after
my reprimand of her that I broke down in tears.

"Of course I mind!" I said. "I don't see you doing this to
anyone else here but my sister. Nicole would hate that you are
doing this to her and to me. Why don't you appreciate people
while they are alive, not when they are dead!"

And with that, they left, finally giving me the chance to
do something that nobody in my family had the opportunity

to do very often: grieve, even if just for a few minutes, like a normal person.

I know it's difficult to imagine, but this is really what life was consistently like. The few examples I gave weren't a few among just a handful. They were a few among thousands. Every single day and in every direction we turned we faced a camera, microphone, reporter, helicopter, newspaper, or some person with a personal interest in, opinion of, or joke about the murder. The rare times when Mom went to the grocery store with Sydney and Justin, she had to first ask an employee to turn the tabloid papers and magazines around at the checkout line so the kids didn't see pictures of their dad or mom with salacious headlines.

When we drove from our home to the funeral at the church, it was like we were on a float in a parade. People were pulling over on the highway to take pictures of us. Overpasses were jammed with curious onlookers. The closer we got to the church, the more crowded the streets were with men, women, and even children who had to be wondering why they were there. People waved, cried, cheered. They all wanted a piece of us; to get close to us. The crowds on the streets were just as large as we drove from the church to the cemetery. Inside the cemetery gates, an endless line of cars stretched along the road that led to Nicole's grave. Reporters, photographers, and videographers were stationed near her grave on top of a brick wall that divided the cemetery from the backyards of some houses. It was as if we were celebrities, but for all of the wrong reasons.

What must Nicole be thinking of all this? I asked myself one day during the trial. She loved her family. She loved her friends. She mostly loved being a mom. She also loved her privacy. But now every phase of her short life was on display to the world.

Many of us often pray that our loved ones who have passed are somehow with us, that their spirits are around us. This was one period of time when I hoped she was enjoying her next life without having any clue of what was going on here. What a mess. And now to top it all off, the man whom most Americans believed sent her and Ron to their graves was about to be set free.

Chapter 12

You Cannot Outrun Your Maker

"I never knew at the time that two people who once loved each other – that one of them could end up killing the other."

– December 8, 2004

O.J.'s double-murder trial lasted more than eight months. To put that in perspective, the high-profile murder trial of Casey Anthony in 2011 in Florida lasted six weeks. Jodie Arias' murder trial in 2013 in Arizona lasted four months. In fact, going back to when jury selection in O.J.'s trial began in September 1994, it actually stretched to more than a year. Opening arguments commenced in January 1995, and the trial ended with the verdict on October 3, 1995.

On May 2, 2013, I was having lunch at a restaurant near my home when I met a very nice couple vacationing from Arkansas sitting at the table next to us. When they learned about my relation to Nicole, they could not stop talking about what they remembered from nearly nineteen years earlier: the Bronco chase, the media attention, the trial, the verdict. They said they even thought about it a few hours before they met me when they passed a white Bronco on the highway. To them it was like it all happened yesterday.

I hear a lot of that when I travel the country for my speaking engagements. People tell me they know where they were when John F. Kennedy was shot in 1963. They know where they were during the 9/11 terrorist attacks in 2001. And they know where they were when the decision came down in the

101

O.J. Simpson trial. I don't see how that is classified with the first two in the realm of American history, but I have accepted the fact that it was just one of those incidents that captivated the world, one that people couldn't let go, and many still can't. I've deleted the need to understand it. Some things just are.

The trial was what many simply labeled "a circus." The evidence against him, on the surface, was so overwhelming, most notably the DNA found at the crime scene that put the chances of anyone but him being the killer somewhere in the range of one in seven billion. There weren't even seven billion people on the planet at that time. But what appeared to many to be an open-and-shut case was anything but that. There was a lot of compelling evidence that was never introduced for various reasons, and defense attorneys hammered witnesses and law enforcement officials on anything and everything they could to put doubts into the jurors' minds. They even made race an issue, claiming that at least one detective in the case was racist and framed O.J.

> *"I told (Prosecutor) Marcia Clark that if justice needed to begin with O.J., a man from within my own family, then so be it. This was NOT a racial issue! Why would people stoop to that level? Society is so closed-minded and bull-headed that people don't want to believe an 'American Hero' is capable of spousal abuse. And his attorneys? I knew they were going to attack us and do what they had to do to get him off."*
>
> – December 13, 2004

The verdict was scheduled to be delivered at about 10 A.M. After a few comments from Judge Lance Ito, it was finally read at 10:07 A.M. It was a very long seven minutes. My hands were sweating, my heart was racing. I was feeling sick to my stomach, worse than what I had felt more than a year earlier going through Nicole's condo. And then it came:

"We the jury in the above entitled action find the defendant, Orenthal James Simpson, not guilty of the crime of murder ... upon Nicole Brown Simpson, a human being ..."

Well, she *was* a human being. The same verdict was read for the charges against him concerning Ron. I was sitting next to my sisters. My parents were a row in front of us. None of them showed any reaction at all. The loudest cries in the room came from Ron's sister, who was sitting a few rows in front of me. I quietly cried, buried my face into the chest of my boyfriend at the time, then asked one of the bailiffs if I could leave.

"I'm sorry, I can't let you out yet," she said with compassion. After a few minutes, once each juror was polled and Judge Ito gave some final instructions, we were allowed to go. We went up to the district attorney's office where I really didn't know what to expect as far as how everyone would behave toward each other, but Mom quickly set the tone.

"OK," she said with no tears or other outward signs of sorrow. "Now we have to focus on the kids." That was Mom – thinking about the welfare of those who needed us, thinking ahead and moving forward, even at a time when she had every right to be angry and think of nobody's well-being except her own.

The strategies used by the defense – the "Dream Team" of lawyers, as they were labeled by the press – worked to perfection. They were able to put enough doubt into the heads of the jurors, never even having to put him on the stand. Whether the means they used to do their jobs justified the end result will be debated forever, but they accomplished what they went there to accomplish. He walked out that morning a free man.

While I remained quiet after the ruling, Denise and my parents were interviewed by Diane Sawyer that afternoon. That was the same interview from which I quoted my dad earlier. My parents were very calm throughout the questioning, refusing to say anything negative about the father of their grandchildren or the judicial process. But Denise's anger toward her former brother-in-law was evident:

"The problem with him is that he is a batterer ... nobody can take that away," she said. "I'm going to continue my fight against domestic violence, and I'm going to put people like him to justice."

When Ms. Sawyer asked my mom what she would remember about Nicole on that day, she said she didn't want to say.

"I will," Denise interjected. "O.J. is going to kill me, and he's going to get away with it. Her words exactly. He's going to kill me, and he's going to get away with it."

As I watch a video of that interview today, I cannot help but think *Wow, that had to feel great for Denise to say all that!* There she was on national television with one of the most prominent and respected journalists of our time, millions of people around the world watching, the perfect platform to speak, and she just let it all out. She spoke from her heart, from her gut, not caring about how anybody would react or how she would be judged. It was what I should have been doing all along. Would it have been enough to snap me out of my depression? Would it have started me on my path to healing ten years sooner? I don't know, but I don't think it could have hurt. *Express It!* – that's one of my twelve tools for beating depression I learned at South Coast that I will discuss later in more depth. Don't keep it bottled up. Make your voice heard.

With that tool in mind as I thought about where to take this chapter and how much to say about the trial, I considered expressing myself by sharing my opinions about all of the players involved – the lawyers, the judge, the witnesses, the experts, specific media members – to let it all out like Denise did twenty years ago. But I realized that I don't need to do that anymore. I've done it already. I've talked out loud to plenty of people in private conversations, in therapy, and even in some media interviews about my thoughts regarding several of those who were linked to the case.

I respect some of those who were involved. Some of them I don't. Some of them said things to our family behind closed doors during the trial that would appall you. But I have no fruitful reason to bring their names or actions up two decades later. I am past all of that and to discuss it now in a book would only be for sensational purposes. Sure, it's tempting, but this is where I need to let go of the *Express It!* tool and bring into play the *Break Free!* tool.

Having already expressed myself over the years for the good of my mental health, I realize now that if I say nothing about those people I do not respect, I remain in control of my emotions. I stay free from the stress and chaos that would ensue if I were to rant with my opinions about them. Imagine what would happen if I did talk about them: the media would read something I wrote about someone, then ask that someone to comment about my comments, and then ask me to comment about that someone's comments about my comments. It would turn into a she said/he said public spat that would create so much stress and chaos for everybody involved, including my family, that who knows how many relationships would be broken. I would lose my authenticity and be no better than those who have profited from my sister's death with their own disreputable comments or books.

The one person I will say something about, though, is O.J. He was the main character in this crime, and I need to bring some closure in this book to the many conflicting thoughts I had about him that fueled my depression.

He was a man I admired growing up, a man I cared for, a man who was family. I initially defended him when people said he killed Nicole, and I fought back my own doubts as the evidence mounted against him. While I know he continues today to deny having anything to do with her murder and the murder of Ron, I know in my heart that he did it. I know that he knows he did it. Some say a lie becomes the truth in your own mind if you tell it enough, but I don't think even his conscience can hide from two brutal murders. If he wants to publicly deny it all the way to his grave, that's fine with me. I honestly do not care. I don't harbor any anger toward him anymore. I really don't.

If he were standing in front of me right now, I truly believe I'd be indifferent toward him. He is not my problem anymore. I believe someone much more powerful than he ever was is waiting for him on the other side of this life, and he will not have a team of high-priced attorneys at his defense to speak for him. He won't be able to lie and get away with it. He won't be able to outrun his maker like he outran defenders on the football field. Nobody is going to be blocking for him. He won't be able to hide in a Nevada prison cell where he was still serving time in 2014 for a robbery he committed in 2007, or on a golf course where he often was when he was free. He will have to face the consequences of his actions for eternity, with no escape or appeals. I can only pray, for his sake, that he repents before that day comes for him.

As much as I am at peace with him today, finding that peace did not happen overnight. It was a very gradual process, one that began on a Sunday morning in church soon after the verdict. No, don't worry, I'm not about to get all religious with you. I simply realized that by forgiving him, I wasn't setting him free – I was setting myself free. Keep reading. No matter what your beliefs are, I am confident you will be able to relate to my point.

CHAPTER 13

FAITH, FORGIVENESS, AND THE GOD OF CRAYONS

"I tried to not let Nicole's death bring me down any more, but it was hard. I faced so much anger, sadness, and loneliness. Finally, I turned to God for help. Even though I had drifted away from Him, He was always there when I went back. He helped me see that I was digging myself the exact same black hole that I dug when Herissa died. So I listened and became still. I became still and realized that I had no control over what happened, and I had to turn it all over to the Lord."

– December 10, 2004

It was a Sunday morning in early 1996, just a few months after the acquittal. My parents and I attended Mass at our usual Catholic church, "usual" meaning whenever we went, and "whenever we went" meaning when Mom felt moved to go. We went each Sunday that Sydney and Justin were with us, including every Sunday during the trial. When they weren't with us, we went maybe weekly, maybe monthly, maybe less frequently than that. No, not devout according to Catholic teachings, but our belief in God always existed, even through our most difficult times. Faith, hope, and love were always the foundation of our home. Prayer was always part of our daily regimen. For whatever reason, though, we just weren't regulars at Mass.

I sat in the pew that morning thinking about the same things I always thought about any time we had attended Mass after Nicole's death: Nicole being in Heaven, her kids, our family, why things happened the way they did, where we were expected to go from here, the everyday things that made me happy and unhappy. What made me most unhappy was what made a lot of people who followed our case unhappy: that the man we believed killed Nicole and Ron was free, while Nicole and Ron were never coming back.

Why do I sit here and think about him every time we come here to church? I wondered. *He's not thinking of me. He doesn't care about us, or how we feel. Where is he right now? Probably on the back nine, trying to figure out whether to use a 9-iron or a pitching wedge. He said he was going to try to find the real killer. I'm pretty sure he isn't putting much effort into that considering we both already know who it is. I know one thing is for sure: he's not wondering what I'm doing right now. So why am I letting him live inside my mind?*

After walking up to receive Holy Communion, I came back to the pew and knelt down. With a hymn playing and providing a rich level of comfort, I folded my hands, bowed my head, closed my eyes, and prayed. I asked God to take care of Nicole and Ron. I asked Him to continue consoling my parents. I asked Him to bless our entire family, especially Sydney and Justin. And then I asked Him for something I hadn't planned to ask for and had never asked Him for previously. It just kind of happened.

"God, we've been through a lot since Nicole's death, and we are going to continue to go through a lot of difficult times. But one thing I don't want any more is to feel the hate that brings me down. Lord, please help me, some way, to forgive him. It feels like what he did to Nicole happened just yesterday. I know the pain of her death will never go away. I can accept that. But please free me of the burden of hate that I have toward him. Please help me to focus on me, my family, not him. No more. I don't want it anymore. Please."

And with that, I felt like I was set free. I lifted my head, opened my eyes, and experienced a comfort that hadn't existed in me since before Nicole died. I'm not saying I went from complete hate to complete forgiveness in a matter of seconds.

But I believe God helped me, at that moment, realize that I was in control of my feelings going forward. The pain of what I believed O.J. did to my sister did not totally evaporate. It never would. But I was no longer going to allow him to control me.

Many times I had asked God to help my family and me through difficult situations. Get us through this day in court. Get us through this interview. Get us through the holidays without Nicole. Get us through this latest accusation about us or Nicole. Get me through this day that I have to pick up Sydney and Justin from their dad. Watch over them when they are with him. But never did I ask God to help me forgive O.J. I had a pretty good idea of how powerful forgiveness could be, of how much freedom it could bring to my mind. I'd heard stories from others, from our pastor during sermons, but I never actually took the time to try it. But it worked. It didn't exonerate him from what he did. It didn't distance me in any way from the spiritual connection I felt I had with Nicole. It allowed me, simply put, to let him go. He would no longer consume me. And by letting him go, it was I who was actually set free.

If you do not believe in God and, as you are reading this, you are saying, "Okay, Tanya, now you're losing me," please stick with me a little longer. Trust me, the last thing I want to do is try to convert you into believing something you don't. I know not everybody believes in God, and I respect that 100 percent. I really do. I have many close friends who don't believe in God. We were all raised differently, come from different backgrounds, and no two of us are alike. But my message to those who do not believe in God is this:

Just believe in *something* or *someone* higher than yourself.

You don't have to be religious about it. You don't have to go to church. The word "God" does not have to be part of your vocabulary. But humbly believe in something or someone greater than you that can be with you, that you can turn to – in your heart and in your mind – so that you are never alone in the battles you are facing.

Sometimes, despite our effort to seek help by turning to others here on earth in our time of need, we still walk away not feeling the emotional support we crave to get us through

it. So if a friend, family member, co-worker, or health professional cannot help us conquer our issue, resulting in us feeling
isolated in what appears to be a hopeless situation, then what?
Faith – faith in something higher – can be all that we have left.
And sometimes it can be all that we need to face and overcome
the challenge before us.

When I was engaged, my fiancé and I went through pre-
marital counseling, as required by my church. That is where I
learned that my fiancé believed in absolutely nothing. Nothing! It was obviously something we'd never discussed because
it completely blindsided me. I knew he didn't go to church. I
knew he didn't follow any particular religion. But it never occurred to me that he didn't believe in any higher power whatsoever.

"What do you mean you don't believe in a higher power?"
I said.

"I just don't," he replied, shrugging his shoulders as if it
were no big deal.

"But you have to believe in something," I implored. I noticed a box of crayons on a shelf in the office we were in at the
counselor's house.

"What about crayons?" I said, pointing at them.

"Huh? What about crayons?" he said confused. Even the
counselor was perplexed.

"Believe in the God of Crayons!" I stressed. We all laughed,
but I had a serious point to make. "Believe in the God of anything. The spirit of anything. The spirit of that desk! Of that
window! Whatever! You just have to believe in something
higher than yourself."

Easier said than done? Maybe not.

I think one of the best ways to find something or someone
higher is to meditate, something I try to practice all the time. It
is part of the valuable *Be Present!* coping tool I learned at South
Coast that I will discuss later in more detail. Meditation, mis-
understood by many who don't do it, can be sitting in silence,
meditating on scripture, doing yoga, listening to a guided im-
agery CD, or doing some deep breathing. It is something you
do by yourself that puts you in a state of calmness, a space of

solitude and peace. It's a place where answers come to you because your mind is still, quiet, and calm. It's a surefire way to shut out the technological distractions of the world and focus. To many, especially in the church, meditation is considered a religion. Yes, meditation can certainly be tied to your faith or to prayer, but it doesn't have to be. It is, in a more general sense, a state of mind – a slowing down of the mind.

Do you ever get a warm, fuzzy feeling when something good happens in your life, something that produces a happiness inside that you just want to hang on to forever? I believe that is a spirit touching and warming your heart. What spirit? Whose spirit? From where? I don't know. For me, it may be God. It may be Jesus. It may be Nicole. Or Herissa. Or Troy. Or my late grandmother. For you, it could be a deceased friend, relative, or even a pet. The point is that believing there is someone or something greater than you, in a place greater than you're in, that can help you across stormy waters, can bring such an amazing sense of peace and comfort.

The key, though, is you have to have the ability to believe. And to do so, you have to open the door of your heart and mind to that spirit. The spirit will always be there knocking, but it's up to you to let it in. Find that meditation comfort zone – the proper time of day, the best location, the best atmosphere. Close out the world – all electronics, all work, all family, all problems, all concerns. Set aside any skepticism you may have about meditation working – that's where the "ability to believe" comes in. Let your mind and heart relax. I think you will be surprised at the powerful, positive effect it will have on your well-being.

As those who already believe in something higher can attest, faith in a higher power can help you rise from a state of depression. It can help you keep life on track and aid you in accepting the unknown and uncertainty that comes with being human. Letting a spirit enter your life will make things a lot easier and more peaceful, especially during turbulent times.

It likely will not be the God of Crayons – but you get my drift.

CHAPTER 14

HELP ME, DON'T RESCUE ME

"How can I stop relying on others to save me all the time and just once and for all be with me, myself, and I? I have to do my part."

– October 25, 2004

There is a very fine line between seeking the necessary assistance and support from other people in order to help us fight our depression and completely relying on others to rescue us from it. If the latter is the mind-set we slip into, which can be easy to do given our vulnerability, the result can be devastating. I learned that the hard way. The really hard way.

While finding the spiritual grace to be able to forgive O.J. in early 1996 was an awesome moment for me in my effort to cope with Nicole's death, it was fleeting. That's because my boyfriend at that time (not to be confused with my ex-fiancé, whom I didn't meet until many years later) robbed me of the faith and hope I had that life would continue getting better.

I met him in September of 1994, just as jury selection in the trial was starting. I was at a club having dinner with some friends when he spotted me. I was wearing an angel pin on my blouse that I'd proudly worn every day for a couple of months in Nicole's memory. He recognized that, and me, as he approached me.

"You're Tanya Brown, right?" he said.

"Yes," I said stunned. He introduced himself.

"I'm so sorry for your loss," he said.

"Wow, thank you," I said with a smile. I was shocked that he knew who I was. We talked for a minute or so; our chat was short since we were both there with other people. But unbeknownst to me at the time, it wouldn't be the last time I would see him. A few months later, soon after the foundation was established, we held our first public benefit at a local concert hall, and there he was. I couldn't believe it. This time, he didn't leave without asking me out first, and I accepted with no hesitation. He was handsome, fun, funny – hilarious actually. So we dated, and it was wonderful. He swept me away. He was the prince charming that every woman wants, always standing up for me, taking me to nice places, buying me nice things, making me laugh. He became my support, my rock, through a very dark time. And I needed that. The more he did for me, the harder I leaned, continually relying on him to keep me afloat emotionally, to prop me up when I was down.

I moved in with him in early 1995. He had seen how cramped my quarters were at home with my sisters and their kids living there, along with Sydney and Justin residing there during the trial. He offered to give me the space I so desperately longed for. It was an opportunity I felt I couldn't pass up given how stressful everything was at home and how kind he had been to me. But as time moved forward, his loving attitude toward me swiftly faded. He became incredibly controlling, needing to always know where I was and what I was doing, turning more into a strict father-like figure to a little girl instead of being an equal partner in an adult relationship.

One day, after a long afternoon in court, we went home and decided to have a barbecue to try to relax. We needed a few things from the store, so I told him I'd go get them. When I arrived there, I ran into a friend whose daughter had recently been murdered. The friend was really struggling emotionally and needed someone to talk to, and who better to talk to than someone in my family? After we spoke for a few minutes and she felt better, I went into the store to buy what I needed, then headed home. When I walked in the door, my boyfriend was waiting for me, and he was piping mad!

"Where were you?" he screamed with every ounce of energy he had.

"What?" I said surprised. "At the store."

"It's been forty-five minutes and the store is only five minutes away!" he yelled. Then he hit me with a barrage of questions: where was I? Why was I gone so long? Who was I with?

"I called the hospital, the police station, and your family to see where you were," he said angrily. We didn't have cell phones back then, so he couldn't call me, but seriously? The hospital and police? As it turned out, no he didn't. He just made that up. I know he did because I checked with my family and he never called them.

And it got much, much worse.

He began working some evenings, so I started spending those nights with my family rather than sitting home alone. He eventually told me he didn't want me doing that. At the same time, he made it clear that he did not want me hanging out with my friends when he was at work. Bottom line: he didn't want me doing anything without him present. The prison he was building around me was shrinking by the day.

The affection that so freely flowed from him when we first met generally disappeared. On two occasions he gave me the silent treatment. One of those times he went three consecutive days without uttering a word to me. I was going stir crazy, with that little hamster in my head spinning the wheel nonstop. *What did I do wrong?* I asked myself. *Did I say something to offend him? If so, what?* He had me so confused that I was apologizing to him, even though I didn't know what for.

I want to be very clear – he never physically hit me – but it felt like his actions were abuse, nonetheless, an emotional abuse that ripped my soul and left me doubting my self-worth. He preyed on my emotional weakness. The trial was draining more and more life out of me every day, and he knew it. I needed support – his support. I needed the Prince Charming I thought he was, but that guy was long gone into the sunset on his white horse. Mom could see his treatment of me devolving, and even said something to me about it. Like many victims of abuse, though, I ignored her wisdom and continued on, displaying my happy face as if everything was fine, hoping things would change – but they did not.

I eventually came to my senses and left him in 1996. What happened between us was his fault. I know that. I had to say that to myself many times to fully realize it, but I know now, under no uncertain terms, that this was all on his shoulders. Where I made a mistake, though, as many people who are suffering from depression and who are under trauma do, was to allow myself to be fully dependent upon him for absolutely everything. Those going through depression and grief are some of the most susceptible to people like him. I wasn't even close to being of sound mind.

So what exactly was I thinking when I latched on to him? A lot of irrational things.

Here was a guy who knew me from all the media coverage of the murder. He didn't think I was Denise. He didn't ask to speak to Denise. He wanted me, not her. Yes, I admit, as silly as it sounds, it was score one for Tanya and not for Denise. That never happened in my life, at least in my mind.

Also, he asked me to move in with him just months after we started dating, getting me out of a loud and crazy house full of people where there was no privacy. He had a beautiful condo with lots of space and peace and quiet. He knew I wouldn't say no to such an offer.

And, to top it all off, I was thinking he really cared about me.

But if relying on others to help me out of depression is necessary, as I mentioned early on, don't I need to trust people? Yes, but not by going all-in with one person and not for the wrong reasons. Why did I pick him? Because I initially fell for his charm without getting to know the real him. Because I was tired of all the chaos in my house and needed to get out. Because I was looking for somebody to rescue me, not help me. All wrong.

The comprehensive lesson to this story is this: if you are suffering with depression, trauma, the loss of someone you love, or an exhaustion that has overwhelmed you, overcoming it begins with you. Yes, you need support. You need others to help you. You need their encouragement. But through it all, you have to be the one to maintain control of your recovery effort. You need help, not a rescue. If you hand your depression and anguish over to another person and say, "Here, take care of this for me," as I did with my ex-boyfriend, there's a good chance you will fall deeper into that sinkhole. Had I known how to maintain control, maybe life would have been better for me much sooner. Instead, my vulnerability to my boyfriend's actions pushed me deeper into depression, a depression that would last for many more years, augmented by Troy's death.

CHAPTER 15

I SENT A BOAT THREE TIMES ...

"Troy had done it and seen it all. Man, if anyone lived life, he did. He was just so extreme in everything he did. But that was Troy. I felt so depressed after his death. I felt dark, lonely, gloomy, gray, negative, just truly empty. I was missing something in my life without him."

– December 10, 2004

Troy was fun. Wild. Dangerous. He lived on the edge, literally. His favorite place was the edge of a cliff where he would begin his graceful flight into the water below. He was a free spirit who did what he wanted, whenever he wanted, and without a care in the world. It's what made him so lovable – but self-destructive at the same time. He showed up at my high school one day, the new kid, and was undoubtedly going to break some hearts. He was cute, witty, cool. Every girl had an instant crush on him. Well, every girl except me. Okay, maybe I sort of liked him. We did try to date once, very briefly, but we knew right away it wasn't going to work. Too awkward. We had way too much fun together to let romance screw it up.

Troy was truly my best friend. I nicknamed him Troylet, and I still crack up thinking about that today. You *have* to be best friends to be able to get away with that. He was part of my family, always at my house, like a piece of the furniture. It wasn't unusual for my family and me to wake up to the aroma of fresh coffee, which he would make after sneaking into our house. He was always there for me, always with a shoulder for me to cry on if I needed it, always cheering me up and making me laugh. One time, soon after we gave up the failed dating experiment, he sent me a dozen roses at work. I called him right away.

"Troy?" I said when he answered. "What the hell?"

"Oh, I guess you got the flowers," he said.

"Yeah, I got them," I snapped in reply. "What did you do that for?"

"I just wanted to tell you that I love you – as a friend, of course," he said laughing. That was Troy, plopping down fifty bucks just to make me smile and brighten my day.

But the riskier side of him, coupled with the sudden death of his father, generated the self-destruction that sent his life into a tailspin.

Troy's dad died unexpectedly in 1988, the year after we graduated from high school. Troy struggled immensely to recover from the void left in his life. He hit the alcohol hard after his dad's death. When he drank, he often ended up in trouble with the law. Three times he was sent to jail, all for relatively minor offenses, but bad situations nonetheless. The first two times a family member bailed him out. The third time nobody did. His family decided it was time for some tough love, and I totally agreed.

He called me from jail soon after his third arrest.

"Can you get me out of here?" he asked, assuming I would.

"Um, no Troy," I said, my voice cracking with sadness.

"What? Why not?"

"People can't keep bailing you out, Troy," I said. "This has to stop."

That was one of the most difficult things I ever had to say to a friend, but I knew it was the right call. When Troy was released after a few days, he went straight to a correctional facility to finish his sentence. His family and I supported him in his effort, and he harbored no ill feelings toward us for him being there. In fact, he was physically and mentally better each time we visited, and the experience at the facility turned him into a new man.

In the years following his release, he started attending church for the first time in his adult life, and he became a born-again Christian. He went away to college and eventually graduated, something that seemed very improbable before he sought help. We didn't keep in close touch during his college years. No reason, other than we were both busy doing our own things, but we had one of those friendships where all it took was one phone call to pick right up where we left off from the last time we talked. That phone call came from him in the spring of 2000. I wasn't available when he called, so he left me a voice mail message to call him right away. He sounded excited in his message, and I returned his call immediately.

"Troy?"

"Tanya! What's going on?" he replied enthusiastically.

"Everything, of course. What's going on with you?"

"You have to guess," he said.

"Uh … you're engaged," I replied, having no idea where that came from. But I was right.

"What? How'd you know?" he asked.

"Just a guess," I said. "That's awesome!"

"She's so wonderful, Tanya," he said. "You're going to love her."

I was thrilled that he'd found true love, a woman who would always be at his side and help him continue living his life on the straight and narrow. Troy and I always had an acute connection with each other emotionally, whether it was the pain of losing his dad, the agony of losing my sister, or the joy of him getting married. If he was happy, I was happy. If I was sad, he was sad. I cannot count how many highs and lows we shared together.

But when it came to the highs, what's the old adage … the higher you rise, the harder you fall? I rose so high with him after he got his life together. I was so happy and proud of all he had overcome. But that level of elation is why what happened in August of 2000 dropped me to a low evocative of Nicole's death.

I was in San Diego handing out fliers at an event for a future fundraiser we were having for the foundation. The day had been such a success that afterward I went to a friend's house just north of San Diego and called Denise to tell her how excited I was about what I had accomplished. After rambling on and on about it, she finally cut me off.

"Tanya, I need you to sit down if you're not already; I need to tell you something," she said somberly. Not the words or tone anybody ever wants to hear; they are never followed by any good news.

Nervous, I sat down.

"What's going on?" I asked.

"Tanya," she said, followed by a deep breath, "Troy died."

I paused for a moment.

"Huh? Troy died?" I said bewildered. I knew a couple of guys named Troy.

"Troy who?" I said.

"Your Troy," she replied.

Another pause.

"What?" I said, in a hushed whisper. "No. No he didn't. No."

But Denise's silence told me otherwise. I broke into tears as Denise cautiously and compassionately gave me details of what happened. Troy had died a couple days earlier while cliff diving with his family at Lake Mohave in Nevada, his favorite place to dive. Mom and Denise kept it from me for so long because they didn't know how to tell me, but they knew they had to eventually. With my years of mental instability, especially after tragic situations, they were worried about how I would react. I wasn't upset with them for that. It was a legitimate concern.

My reaction to his death was different from my reactions to the deaths of Nicole and Herissa because of the manner in which he died. I knew who was responsible for Nicole's death. I blamed the hit-and-run driver, though never found, for killing Herissa. Troy's death, however, was a total accident. But as I went through the grieving process, I looked for someone to blame … and I chose God.

"How can You do this?" I said angrily to Him while lying in bed crying later that night. "He found You, he found a wonderful companion whom he was going to marry in three months, he went to college, he stopped drinking. He completely straightened out his life. And now You just rip all of that away from him?"

I was becoming more and more livid.

"He was only thirty! Why would You do that?"

Even though I'd dealt with such heartbreaking losses previously, this was the first time I ever recalled questioning my faith. I didn't lose it, but Troy's death raised a lot of questions in my head as to what my purpose was here on earth. What was anybody's purpose? If someone like Troy could bounce back the way he did, do everything the right way, and still lose it all, what was the point of anything?

Over the next couple of weeks, I fell back into the languor I'd become accustomed to so many times after such tragedies. I couldn't sleep. I couldn't get out of bed in the morning. I had no desire to do anything at all. Somehow, one day Mom was able to coax me into going shopping with her. It was September 7, to be exact, just a couple weeks removed from Troy's funeral. I remember the date because it was the birthday of a friend of mine, which Mom reminded me about.

"You should call her," Mom said.

"No, I don't want to," I mumbled. I could feel myself slowly becoming the Tanya who materialized after Herissa died. But Mom was not about to go through that again. This time around, she took a more direct approach with me.

"You know what," she said. "Go over to Troy's house and talk to his mom," she said.

"About what?" I said.

"About him. About how they're doing. Whatever. Just go confront this now. Go over there tonight and talk to her," she said.

"I don't …"

"Do it!" she said, cutting me off in mid-sentence.

At 6:30 P.M., without giving Troy's mom and stepdad any notice that I was coming, I knocked on their door. I had no idea what I was going to say, or how I would respond to anything they said, but I knew Mom was right. I needed to confront what I was feeling, and who better to do that with than the people who were probably grieving more than I was? While I didn't know what to expect them to look like when they answered, I guess I had a general assumption that they would not look well. Perhaps they might look like they'd been sobbing nonstop since the funeral and wouldn't want to talk to anybody, including me. But when they opened the door, I found the opposite to be true, and I was shocked.

"Hi Tanya!" they said with big smiles, obviously thrilled to see me.

Oh my gosh! I thought. *Their son just died, yet look at them!* I couldn't believe what I was witnessing.

> *"'What are you guys taking?' I asked them, 'Because you look so at peace.' I am so dark, sad, mad over his loss. I mean, here is a guy who had so many trials and tribulations, found God, got engaged, and then died. I proceeded to tell them that he was their kid, he was my friend, and I want what they have because right now I am so lost and dark – I don't know where to turn. They told me that what they were taking was the Holy Spirit. 'Then give it to me. I want some!' I said. They prayed over me, and it was at that very moment of surrendering all to Him that I felt warm and cozy inside. I no longer felt alone, afraid, dark. I felt warm. Seriously warm, as though someone just gave me a huge bear hug. It filled me with peace, joy, love, and light."*
>
> – December 10, 2004

It was one month later that I found a non-denominational church I liked and was eventually baptized. That was when I stopped blaming God for what happened to Troy. I deleted the need to try to understand why Troy died and realized that it just was, that everything happens for a reason, even if I don't immediately know what that reason is.

But that didn't automatically make everything all better.

I've heard stories about people who found their faith, got baptized, and instantaneously became completely different people. I know that can happen, and it's certainly a good thing. It even happened to Troy to an extent. But speaking as someone who had been suffering from depression for a decade at that point, my newfound faith didn't completely fix me. Yes, it helped. It helped a lot. As I stated earlier, I believe we all need to lean on something or someone higher than ourselves. For me, that is God, and I know I would struggle to function without Him in my daily life. But at the same time, I do not believe those of us with depression can expect prayer and God to instantly make everything better. There has to be effort on our part. An effort to rehabilitate. An effort to change.

I am reminded of the old joke about a man who was in his home when a flood rose to the level of his front porch. A guy in a boat came by to rescue him, but the man refused to go.

"I've been praying to God," the man said to the boat driver. "Go on. God will take care of me."

A little while later, with the flood rising and the man hanging out his second-story window, the guy in the boat came by again.

"Nope, I'm good," the man in the house said. "God will save me."

The flood continued to rise, forcing the man onto the rooftop. The man in the boat came by once more, only to be denied again.

When the flood finally consumed the house, the man in the house drowned. When he got to Heaven, he confronted God about what happened.

"Why did You let me die?" the man said. "I put my faith in You. I thought You would save me."

"Are you kidding me?" God replied. "I sent a boat three times to rescue you. What more did you want?"

Several messages can be harvested from that joke. What I take from it is that while prayer is certainly good and while counting on God or whatever higher source of power we have in our lives is good, we also have to work at solving our problems ourselves. We have to open our ears and listen, open our minds and think, recognize and take advantage of help when it's there, dig our feet in deep, roll up our sleeves, and work hard to accomplish what we want.

I believe God worked through my mom by having her suggest I go see Troy's parents. I believe He worked through Troy's parents by showing me the power of the Holy Spirit. I believe He worked through Mini the day I snapped – I was stranded in a flood of depression, and she came by in a boat and said "Let's go." That led me to South Coast, where God would work through the staff there to help me heal ... but only as long as I was willing to help myself.

If you have never been inside a psychiatric unit, it looks a lot like any other floor in a hospital. Doctors roam the halls. People are medicated. Patients are there with the common purpose of getting well. The primary difference is that the wounds aren't as easy to see in a psych unit, and they require a certain special care – from others and from within oneself – that a bandage cannot fix.

CHAPTER 16

I DON'T WANT TO DIE

"I am tired of fighting with everybody. I am tired of being depressed. I don't like being locked up, but I know I have to be here. I guess one day at a time, as they say. My oh my, how did I snap? This is my question."

– October 11, 2004

When I checked into South Coast, I had to fill out a considerable amount of paperwork, including a lengthy questionnaire. There were eighteen questions to answer, along with a list of nine goals I had to prioritize by ranking them from most important (one) to least important (nine). I also had to check off the coping skills (based on a list they gave me) with which I felt I needed help.

I know there may be nothing more boring than reading medical records, especially those of someone else. For that reason, I am not going to share every piece of the dozens of documents recorded about my depression. But I do want to share a few interesting ones that will give you a better understanding of my mentality throughout my recovery process, help you better understand some compelling stories that follow, and give you a sense of what happens behind those mysterious doors of a psych unit.

The good news is that because I had time at Deana's parents' house to decompress after I snapped at home, I felt free to be myself and speak my mind when I filled out the paperwork. I didn't hold back any of my thoughts or feelings. I really wanted to get better and knew that being completely honest was the only way to do it. For the first time in nearly fifteen years, I was as authentic as I could be.

Here is a look at the questionnaire I had to complete. Notice how blunt the questions were, from "Why do you want to change?" to "Do you have feelings of hopelessness?" to "Do you want to die?" That straightforwardness from them gave me the feeling that they wanted to help me as much as I wanted to be helped.

1) Please describe your daily schedule (at home) with the approximate time you get up.

   I get up at 9 or 9:30. I sit with my family, have coffee, play with the dogs, and go back to bed to avoid noise, unsolicited advice, and to just avoid feeling.

2) How do you handle conflict with others? Give an example.

   Usually I am OK. I stand up for myself. But lately I scream and yell and get so angry. For example, yesterday I flipped out on my sister. Anything will trigger me.

3) Please rate your ability to relax on your own from 1 to 10, with 1 being deeply relaxed and 10 being highly anxious.

   Seven.

4) What is your main career?

   Trying to get my speaking career up and running. I speak on domestic violence issues.

5) State your goals for the future (i.e. work, school, volunteering).

   Want to finish my B.A. in sociology, give back to my community somehow, get married, be self-sufficient.

6) What leisure interests do you do alone or with others?

   Nothing really. I am a homebody. I may read my Bible, journal, play with my dogs, or sleep.

7) State your goals for leisure and social outlets.

   I want to wake up, be happy, exercise and just love life.

8) What do you feel are your present personality strengths?

   Compassionate, generous, sincere, loving, caring, giving, sympathetic, understanding.

9) Why do you want to change?

   Because right now I am 34 and I don't want to rely on anyone or anything to make me happy.

10) Would you describe your relationship with your family to be close, distant or indifferent?

    Close.

11) Would you describe your relationship with your friends to be close, distant or indifferent?

    Close.

12) Do you have feelings of hopelessness? If yes, explain.

    I feel everything I do falls apart. What am I meant to be doing when my heart says "help people?" It's such a struggle.

13) Do you have feelings of isolation? If yes, explain.

    Right now, yes. Just want to be left alone. I sleep a lot so I don't have to deal with anything.

14) Do you like where you are living?

    I love living with my family, but too many strong personalities. It all gets to me. I could move in with my ex, but I don't like that either. Help!

15) What are your plans one year from now?

    I was planning on marrying on 9-11-04 and one week before, he canceled. He is working on his issues and I'm working on mine. I do hope we'll be together. I also want to put out effort with courage to pursue my degree and speaking.

16) What are your plans five years from now?
    Write my life story to help others overcome adversity.

17) Do you want to die?
    No.

18) Can you make a verbal contract not to harm yourself?
    Yes.

19) Please prioritize your goals for this hospitalization.
    (this is the order I put them in)

    1. Improve problem-solving abilities.

    2. Develop and maintain physical strength and endurance.

    3. Channel feelings into constructive outlets.

    4. Improve use of leisure time.

    5. Improve self-esteem.

    6. Improve communication skills.

    7. Find ways to relax.

    8. Improve social skills.

    9. Improve body image.

20) Check the style(s) of ineffective coping that best fit
    you. *(below are the ones I checked)*

    *Anxiety, depression, interpersonal problems, loss of func-
    tioning with unexpected obstacles, low self-confidence and
    give up easily, poor self-reliance, inaccurate self-perception,
    and obsessive-compulsive.*

21) Additional comments:

    *I don't want to die. But sometimes when life has been so dif-
    ficult and sad you do say "I want to die." But I talk about it
    with my parents and sister, Mini. I would never do it. I just
    get so depressed and hopeless.*

One more form I had to fill out was a suicide assessment, one of the most humbling things I've ever had to do. Some of those questions I answered on the previous questionnaire weren't easy to answer, but when you then receive a form with questions specifically about your intent to end your life, it opens your eyes wide to the seriousness of where your life is. Most of the questions on it were yes or no questions, such as "Do you have a suicide plan?" (No) and "Does your family have a history of suicide attempts?" (No). But two other questions opened the door for me to speak up for the first time about the losses in my life. That was my initial acknowledgement that I had not come to terms yet with those losses.

Question: Do you have any suicidal ideas?
My answer: *My life has always been difficult/challenging. I have experienced a ton of loss. I speak about not wanting to be here, but I know life gets better. I have no plan!*

Question: Have you suffered any recent losses?
My answer: *Where do I start? My sister was murdered ten years ago. My best friend (Herissa) died. My friend (Troy) died.*

Looking today at those answers, as simple as they were, I think they told a couple of tales: one is that those losses of life were still deeply affecting me, even though Herissa's death was fifteen years earlier and Nicole's was ten. The other was that I seriously wanted to confront the pain of those losses. I did not want to kill myself. At least I didn't think I did. I had no suicide plan. I knew life could get better. I just didn't know what I needed to do to make it better. That's why I was there.

After some more evaluations, I was officially diagnosed with major depressive disorder. It was a toxic mix of sadness, anger, low self-esteem, and an abundance of other pessimistic feelings and emotions that had to be dissolved.

CHAPTER 17

WORK WITH ME, OR I CAN SLAM YOU

"I read a passage from Proverbs today that I think I need to learn from, but it's so hard: 'He who loves a quarrel loves sin. He who builds a high gate invites destruction.'"

– October 14, 2004

I slid into a wheelchair after check-in and was rolled to my room on the second floor with no idea what to expect. I envisioned the old mid-twentieth century stereotype of a mental ward that was often portrayed in movies – a group of zombie-looking people shuffling around aimlessly through colorless hallways, moaning and pointing with little functionality. But I had to keep reminding myself that I was one of them now. I was no longer an outsider looking in. This was going to be my home for the next ten days and then for another couple of months every day as an outpatient. This was where I belonged. And you know what? It was nothing like that description I just gave. I could function. I was no zombie. At least I didn't feel like one.

When we arrived, I was underwhelmed, which was a good start. Nothing jumped out at me as creepy or scary. Everything looked normal, like an office building, or maybe even a school. As we started down the long carpeted hallway, a large, bright, open room with huge windows, couches, and chairs was on my immediate left. That was the group meeting room. Next to that was a similar-sized room that served as the cafeteria. There was a phone on the wall in the hall right outside the cafeteria. Patients could use it to make or receive calls – first-come, first-served since it was the only one. Down a little further on the right were showers, and at the end of the hall on the right was the main nursing station like one would see on any floor in a regular hospital.

On the left, across from the nursing station, was the beginning of a semi-circular hallway. That's where the patient rooms were. Mine, room 214, was about one third of the way down the hallway and looked like a typical hospital room – two twin beds (I did not have a roommate), white walls, white tiled floor, large windows, and a private bath. There was no mirror in the bathroom thereby alleviating any chance of a patient shattering it in order to do harm. Overall, my first impression was a good one. My room was actually bigger than my room at home. I had space that I'd never had before.

The key starting block for my path to recovery was structure. Everything South Coast had me do was painstakingly organized to the max. I had to wake up at the same time every morning, eat my meals in the same room and at the same time every day, take my medications at the same time each day (I will delve more into medications a little later), and attend individual and group sessions. Visitors, who usually included Mom, Dad, Mini, and my ex-fiancé, had a specified one-hour window each evening to see me. Keeping a strict schedule was critical. It helped keep down-time to an absolute minimum and left little time for me to worry about things.

At least that was the intention.

My second day there I was in the cafeteria eating lunch when the community phone in the hallway rang. One of the women who was expecting a call jumped up to answer it. She came back in the room after a few seconds looking glum. It wasn't for her.

"Tanya, it's for you," she said.

"Me? Who is it?" I wasn't expecting a call from anybody.

"I don't know," she said, sitting back down to finish eating.

Feeling suspicious, I walked into the hall. I guess maybe it could have been Mom or Mini.

"Hello?"

"Tanya Brown?" It was a man, not my dad or my ex.

"Yes."

When he told me who he was, I nearly dropped the phone.

"What?" I said stunned. "You can't be serious! How did you know I was here?"

"I have my sources," he said with a chuckle. "Listen, I'm going to write a story about you being in there. You can either work with me, or I can slam you. It's up to you."

What marvelous choices. He was a reporter with the *National Enquirer*.

When it came to the media, my family dealt with all kinds of personalities. A few of them attempted to build relationships with us by being kind in their questioning, respecting our privacy when we asked, and not overstepping moral boundaries. Most were rude and aggressive – out to make a name for themselves, grab higher ratings, or beat their competition – without any consideration for the pain we were suffering. Despite the fact that *National Enquirer* reporters probably have a reputation more in line with the latter, this particular reporter fell somewhere in the middle. I would classify him as one of the nicer ones who showed some care and concern toward our family in the past. But when he got the scoop that I was at South Coast … well, you saw the two no-win choices he gave me.

I was literally shaking, part of it nervousness and part of it anger. I was upset that the reporter was doing this to me, but even more upset that someone told him I was there. Who did it? It could have been anyone – a friend who heard about it from someone in our family, another patient at the hospital, or a family member of a patient who visited and saw me there.

I learned throughout the trial that money can talk louder than ethics or morals, and obviously someone was more concerned about making a buck by providing the reporter with a tip about my whereabouts than thinking of the potential effect such a story could have on me. But that was pretty much the way it was ten years earlier, and I had no reason to expect people had changed. I wanted to run into the cafeteria and scream "Who told him?" but many of the other patients did not yet know my relationship to Nicole. I was stuck holding on to my anger, except for what I could take out on the reporter without causing too much commotion.

"Are you really going to do this to me?" I asked him in a harsh whisper.

"I'm just doing my job," he said, a standard reporter reply. "C'mon, it won't be that bad."

Easy for someone on his end to say. I paused for a moment, trying to come to terms with the fact that I was trapped. I couldn't lie; he knew where I was. I made a quick decision to just get it over with.

"I guess I'll have to work with you," I mumbled reluctantly.

"Great!" he replied. And I did the interview right there on the spot. I couldn't believe it. I was standing in the hallway of the psych ward doing an interview with the *National Enquirer*.

For the rest of that day and the next, my stress levels soared. I thought I was coming into South Coast to minimize my issues. Instead, just two days in, my anxieties were compounded with this story hanging over my head. The daily medical log the workers there kept on me reflected my angst.

"10/14/04 ... Upset because she found out that the *Enquirer* (tabloid) will print a sensational story about her tomorrow saying she 'flipped out' and ended up coming in here."

I couldn't concentrate or sleep a wink. I gave the interview the best that I could, trying to be rational about everything, but it was the *National Enquirer,* where printing the whole truth often appeared to be optional. My situation was about to be exposed to the world, a world of people who relied on that tabloid for their news. I fretted about it in my private therapy sessions, where I was introduced to one of the first coping tools, which I call *Accept and Surrender!* It is basically a secular way of saying "Follow the *Serenity Prayer*." Or a catchier way of saying "Some things just are." I learned that no matter how upset I became, there was nothing I could do about the story. The reporter was going to write what he wanted to write, and it was going to print no matter what. With time, it would be overshadowed by the next "big story." Until then, I had to accept it and surrender to it.

I had someone buy me a copy and bring it in to me when it ran later that week. I sat on my bed and opened it up and there it was. My first reaction was, as expected, panic. The headline was loudly displayed in large, black, bold letters: "Simpson sends Nicole's sister to mental hospital" with a goofy photo of him smiling below it. They also used a couple of file photos – one of Nicole and one of me with Mini. The first line of the story mimicked the headline: "O.J. Simpson has driven his ex-wife Nicole's sister into a mental hospital!" Well, that's not exactly what happened. And the exclamation point, which was obviously some forced emphasis for an attempt at a dramatic effect, made me laugh. I tentatively read the story, anticipating a line or word that would set me off. But it never came.

I will give the reporter credit – he kept his word, as the story certainly came across more as a collaboration than a "slam." I went from feeling panic to feeling a bit of relief. It wasn't a bad story. He threw in some of his own narrative, which was fairly accurate, and he also captured my voice pretty well.

"I had a mental breakdown and I checked myself into a hospital to get better," he quoted me as saying. "I've suffered a lot of loss in my life and I never really dealt with it." I also said O.J.'s actions "scarred me for life" and that I would likely be dealing with it for as long as I lived.

As traumatic as a story like that could have been to me at that time, I think it turned out to be one of the many turning points in my healing. It forced me to open up publicly, to have no secrets with anyone about what I was going through, and to candidly share a little bit about depression. But what was most important to me was how I reacted to the reporter finding me. I was initially terrified, but then took the hand I was dealt and made something good, or at least something not so bad, come out of it. I proved to myself that I really could take what appeared on the surface to be a negative situation and turn it into something better. I accepted and surrendered, and it worked.

This was just a tiny step in what was going to be a very long journey. But at least I seemed to be heading in the right direction.

CHAPTER 18

THE BUTTERFLY

"I haven't slept regularly in five days. My body and mind are very tired. I also feel bored. I don't feel like looking or reading. I have a guilty feeling for not being able to motivate myself and for having difficulty concentrating. I'm out of my element here, I guess. I don't want to talk to anyone. It's all too exhausting."

– October 16, 2004

My private therapy sessions were with two different social workers who were integral in my recovery. They made me feel comfortable right out of the gate, and I felt like I could tell them anything. I opened up about my issues with Denise and my ex-fiancé, my feeling that Mini was really the only one in my family who understood what I was going through, some problems I had with other patients there who negatively stimulated me with their erratic behavior, and, of course, the *National Enquirer* tracking me down. I talked and cried and laughed throughout the sessions, taking the social workers with me on one heck of a temperamental ride, but it was probably nothing they weren't used to.

They listened and took copious notes each session which, as I read them now, prove how severely unstable I was. Words and phrases they and I used to illustrate my volatile moods during my ten days there included "I'm learning a lot here," "I'm angry," "I'm scared," "I feel energized," "She is pleasant and compliant," "Her mood is depressed," "She remains motivated," "She remains fragile," and "She is very hopeful of getting a positive result 'one day at a time.'" Those weren't necessarily comments from one day to the next. Sometimes they were from the same session, from negative to positive and back again; all over the board and beyond. This is how depression messes with you. You try and try and try to find the good around you because you want to be happy, but one bad moment, one bad memory – that one trigger – can smother your sincere intentions and stifle you into thinking that all hope has vanished.

Trigger. There's another very popular word used in the realm of depression. In the simplest terms, it's something that stimulates a reaction. While I've used the word in a positive way, such as when I said Mini's intervention after I blew up at my family triggered the start of my healing, the word generally has a negative connotation. For example, Irwin said something in regard to his numerology that triggered my explosion; Herissa's death triggered my depression; Denise said something to trigger my anger and frustration. A trigger is something you know is out there, and you try to consciously avoid for your mental well-being, but it's not easy to do. When it rears its ugly head, it can be suffocating.

That is where the private sessions helped. They gave me a safe place where I could talk about those triggers and say what I wanted about whomever or whatever I wanted with the comfort of knowing that it would stay in that room. When the *National Enquirer* triggered my emotions, I said many choice words about them, the reporter, the media in general, the people who read that newspaper. It was a great stress-reliever, and the more I released, the better I knew I would feel in the long run. That is why I always strongly encourage people to not only talk about their issues out loud, but to talk about them out loud when they surface rather than holding them in for any extended period of time.

The inpatient group sessions were very different from the private ones, as one might imagine. Each session was optional for everyone, and class sizes were usually small. Though patients were strongly encouraged to go, not everybody on the floor did. One reason was a rule that if you came and then left for any reason, even to go to the bathroom, you weren't allowed back in. There was that structure. Another reason was people were intimidated to share their problems with strangers, especially strangers who had their own problems. Me? I was ready to open up to anyone. Even if it meant I might pee in my pants in the middle of a session, there was no way I was going to miss one. Hearing stories from others in situations similar to mine helped me more than someone lecturing about how I should behave, and I never held back what was on my mind. We each had serious problems, so I saw no reason for me not to be honest.

"She's very verbal about herself," the leader of our class wrote in my log on October 14 after our group session. "She was allowed to talk, expressed her feelings, and it was a supportive environment. She verbalized that she is very motivated to go straight despite everything that has happened to her. Immediate future plans are to get treatment."

Each class was different. We had different topics and different ways of tackling those topics. For example, we would occasionally create collages, which experts say tap into the subconscious mind, finding things about yourself that the conscious mind doesn't pick up. One of our first assignments was to go through magazines and cut out pictures we were attracted to, pictures that gave a sense of where our lives were at the time. I cut out a photo of a guy and girl. The girl looked a little like me. The guy had the same name as my ex-fiancé.

In another class, we worked on a stress situation worksheet. My answers to the questions on it were very telling of where my mind was:

Question: What is one very stressful situation in my life right now?
My answer: *My ex is my stress, anger and depression trigger.*

Question: How am I handling it?
My answer: *I keep talking to the man.*

Question: How would it look if it were resolved?

My answer: *I would not speak to him during my recovery so I can see my life more clearly.*

Question: What can I do to reduce the stress?

My answer: *Exercise, eat right, think of me and what's good for me. Get in tune with nature. Continue with a gratitude journal. Look at my strengths and positives that I possess. And choose not to have my ex in my life.*

It became obvious, through those two classes and subsequent ones, that my ex was my biggest immediate issue that needed to be addressed. He was in my mind all the time. He visited me often, which was nice of him, but we usually ended up arguing about something when he was there. The sight of him kept taking me back to that awful day when our engagement broke down, mainly because he was still the same person. I would use my therapy sessions during the day to release some of the lingering stress I felt from our breakup. But then he would come in to visit in the evening and his presence would create new stress, and I'd have to start all over in therapy the next day. It may have been different if he had come in one of those nights and said, "Forget the prenup, let's get married." But he didn't. He was the same person. I was the same person ... getting help, but still depressed from issues that existed long before I met him. I was a long way from overcoming it.

> "He complains about how his bank account has dwindled away since we met (ring, wedding, clothes). I am also fearful of working for him now because of all this lack of trust. What if we divorce? I would've been working with him during our marriage, but then bye-bye, what job do I have? He thinks speaking gigs come up for me all the time, but then he wants me home at the same time. And why does he want me to move in with him so bad? I'm so confused and scared of these issues. I'm going to &*#%*$@ snap again! I feel pressure. I don't need this!"

– October 13, 2004

Those impulsive feelings of confusion and pressure, along with the fear of snapping, are what make depression so difficult for people who suffer from it to explain, and for those who have never gone through it to comprehend. It's not like catching a cold, trudging through it for a few days, recuperating and staying better for the next twelve months until you catch another cold. It's never that easy, not even close. It comes and goes when it wants – by days, hours, or minutes. You could feel really good about something, then a trigger will suddenly emerge and swing you the opposite way. How quickly you quash that trigger can depend on your available support at the time, or on your self-motivation, which may be difficult to garner depending on what else you've had to deal with recently.

John Milton, author of *Paradise Lost*, wrote in that epic poem: "The mind is its own place, and in itself can make a Heaven of Hell, a Hell of Heaven." I can't describe depression any better than that.

A little less than halfway through my inpatient therapy, around October 14 or 15, during one of my darker hours with my ex primarily on my mind, I was sitting quietly on the edge of my bed facing the wall of windows and staring at the sunset that was about to turn the day into dusk. I was thinking about how much negativity, much of it revolving around him, was being flushed out of me in my individual sessions, my group sessions, and my journaling. I knew that was okay and normal. That was part of what all of those therapies were for – to discharge those emotions – but they were consuming more of my days than I expected, or at least it felt that way, because that negativity was so plentiful and powerful.

I don't feel like this is working, I muttered in my mind. *I'm trying, at least I think I am. I want to get better. But how soon until I start seeing the good from all this? I know it's only been a few days, but it feels so much longer. I'm tired. My soul is tired. I don't know how much more I can take.*

Mini popping into my room at just the right moment the day I snapped at home proved how critical timing and support can be in turning any situation around. And it happened to me again that evening at South Coast as I gazed out the window at the sunset. Out of nowhere, fluttering outside in mid-air, was a beautiful black and yellow butterfly. It was gracefully waving its wings, looking right at me, then gently landed on the ledge. I stood up and walked toward the delicate creature. It never flinched, unafraid of my presence. Maybe it knew I couldn't open the window.

Or maybe it was making sure it had my attention.

Once my eyes were glued to it, the butterfly lifted itself from the ledge and flew into the sunset. I followed it until it was far enough away that I could no longer see it. But when it was out of sight, a whole new world opened up to my eyes. For the first time since I'd arrived at South Coast, I noticed the beauty of the Pacific Ocean. *Wow!* I thought to myself. *What a view!* Yes, it was the same ocean that was just a couple blocks from my house my entire life, but I guess I'd taken its splendor for granted. It was a pristine evening. I looked to the right and could see all the way to Palos Verdes, then looked to the left and could see San Diego in the distance.

"This is incredible," I gasped out loud. "Just incredible!"

I noticed leaves blowing in the breeze and a dog scampering freely in the backyard of a home. I saw the waves crashing, the sandy beach, the beautiful foliage. All that beauty had been there my whole life, but it was never as obvious to me as it was at that moment. I knew immediately that this had to be a sign. A sign that there really was a lot of good out there; I just needed to always keep my eyes and mind open to it, no matter what trigger tried to get in the way. I needed to always remain open to the possibilities that lie ahead for me. I felt relief. I felt light. I felt motivated to move on.

That butterfly …

Why did it pick my window at precisely that time when I was in that mood? Why did it take the path it did as it flew away, pulling my eyes behind it toward the ocean? I wanted to know, but I also knew I would never find the answer. I just had to trust that there was a reason, one that involved me moving forward. It was a moment I could not afford to let go.

I turned away from the window and scrambled to get my binder of papers from my therapy sessions that week. I pulled out a worksheet we'd done about how to say "no" to people which, of course, could reduce stress in our lives considerably. According to the worksheet, "*No* is a solid shield against manipulation. *No* informs and educates the other party about what is acceptable and what is not. *No* teaches others how to treat us. *No* identifies ownership." One question on the worksheet asked, "How has your *yes* affected you when it should have been a *no*? What damage has it brought to you?" The answer I wrote:

My ex's proposal. A broken heart, trust issues. I was betrayed. Ended up in the hospital. Even before that, when he asked me out, I had the gut feeling he wasn't "right." Saying no would have saved me a lot of struggles. This all brings me a clearer understanding of myself.

A couple days later, after another tense visit from my ex and more therapy, it all finally clicked – he had to go. Not just for a while. Not just until I needed someone to talk to, like the night I called him from Deana's parents' house after snapping at home. But for good. We had learned that week about the coping tool I mentioned earlier called *Break Free!* and I knew that I needed to permanently disengage from him. He was a major piece of the stress and chaos in my life. Yes, I loved him. I wanted to marry him because he had a lot of wonderful qualities. But I knew there was no way I could. It would be a horrible marriage. As obvious as that may have seemed to some as soon as he handed me the one-sided prenup, it was not that vivid to me. I needed the tools, the group sessions, the worksheets, the journaling – the butterfly – to figure it out.

Through more therapy sessions, I determined that overcoming depression was much like trying to solve a math problem involving big numbers, but without the use of a calculator. I couldn't just punch in numbers and have the answer instantly spit out at me; I had to do it the long way with a pencil, paper, and an eraser. I needed to break each number down to the basics and do the individual steps. I couldn't glaze over anything. No shortcuts. It would be frustrating at times. Sometimes it would feel like the answer was never going to come, but whatever it took, however long it took, getting to the result through the long and tedious method was the only way I was going to get better, and ultimately stay better.

> *"I truly feel that my ex needs me more than I need him now. This guy is not ready for relationships or marriage. He treats me like a business deal. Well you know what? I am not a business deal! I have a unique spirit, a loving heart, and he doesn't deserve me. So I took him off my calling and visiting list at the hospital, so now I can finally heal."*

– October 19, 2004

It would take several more weeks for me to completely disconnect from my ex emotionally for good, but knowing that he could no longer visit me or make contact with me for my remaining couple of days there as an inpatient was a huge catalyst for me. It was the first major sign for me since I'd been at South Coast that I was starting to take control of my life.

I know my ex to this point has not been portrayed in the best light, but I would be remiss if I didn't point out some of the wonderful qualities about him. While he was very serious about his business, he also knew how to have fun. We truly enjoyed life with each other when we were together, and he was very much a gentleman. In fact, after he broke off our engagement and it was obvious that I could no longer continue to work for him, he kept me as an employee long enough for my hospital stay to be covered by his insurance. He knew I needed help, and it was a no-brainer for him to do that for me.

Rather than being a bitter ex-bride-to-be, I look today at what happened then as a blessing. His canceling the wedding was hands down the most difficult thing to endure because it brought every ounce of pain to the surface, but it was needed for me to be able to address that pain and move forward with my life. Everything happens for a reason, and we are both better people today for what happened.

If the depression I was experiencing when I let him go for good was a math problem involving two 10-digit numbers, I was still only on step one toward solving it. But I was getting it. I was breaking it down. I was learning how to do it. And the staff there noticed. I was close to being "promoted," if you will, to the outpatient program. I just needed to continue staying focused on working toward the ultimate solution.

Our last family photo with Nicole was taken at our home on Mother's Day in 1994, about a month before she was killed. From left: Nicole, Dominique, Denise, Mom, Dad, and me.

I always felt like I had a lot to live up to with such beautiful sisters. That's Dominique, Nicole, and me.

I got O.J. a lighter for one Christmas in the late 1970s (Mom and Dad bought it and gave it to me to give to him). I don't think he smoked, but it was more of a nostalgic piece that matched a backgammon table we bought him.

Kato Kaelin, a witness in the trial, was one of Nicole's good friends and was loved by Sydney and Justin so much that they named their dog after him. This is me with Kato, who lived with us after Nicole's death. He died in 2004 while I was being treated at South Coast for my depression.

Herissa was so beautiful and always so happy. She was twenty-six when she was killed. (Photo by Douglas Miller)

An awesome photo of Troy. Standing high on a mountaintop with his backpack, it not only reflects his adventurous side, but symbolizes just how much he was on top of the world after putting his life back together. (Photo by Sonja Axelson Johnson)

This is one of my favorite photos of Nicole, taken shortly before her death. It was not easy finding photos of her since she was usually the one taking the pictures. She left behind eighty photo albums.

Nicole loved to shop. This was one of our shopping trips when we went to San Francisco on a short vacation for some quality sister time.

This was taken when I was a teenager at a restaurant owned by some friends of our family. From left: Denise, me, Dominique, and Nicole.

During the trial, there was an artist in the courthouse named Robert Wayne who created that picture of Nicole with crayons. When he was finished, he gave it to our family. It now hangs in our living room. From left: Me, Mom, Dad, Dominique, and Denise.

Mom and Denise picked out Nicole's gravestone with the simple, yet eloquent, message of "Always in our hearts." Nicole is buried in Ascension Cemetery in Lake Forest, California, near our grandparents.

This is Nicole's Tiffany lamp that I accidentally knocked off the table in my bedroom on October 9, 2004, the day I snapped. It still sits in the same place today, on a table at the foot of my bed. The broken glass shade serves as a daily reminder of where I once was and how far I've come.

South Coast Medical Center, which is now Mission Hospital Laguna Beach, was instrumental in helping me save my life. I was admitted there in October 2004 and discharged in late December that same year.

I finally earned my master's degree in Counseling Psychology from Argosy University in October 2013, seven years after earning my bachelor's degree in the same field, and twenty-six years after graduating from high school.

This family photo was taken in 2013 in the courtyard of our home. From left: Dominique, Leslie Carr Roney (Dad's granddaughter from his first marriage), Mom, Denise, Aiden Roney (Leslie's daughter), Dad, and me.

Denise, me, and Dominique each tossed a rose into the Pacific Ocean the evening of June 12, 2013, the nineteenth anniversary of Nicole's death. We held public vigils annually during the first fifteen years, but have since held private vigils in this manner.

CHAPTER 19

MY NEW PERSPECTIVE

"I recognized upstairs (inpatient) that I was anxious to be discharged. I was so relieved when my doctor said I'm going to PHP (Partial Hospitalization Program, or outpatient program). PHP is helping me, giving me the courage to look at everything with a clear picture. I'm not so animated or expressive anymore. That was so exhausting. The doctor told me I need to learn to contain my emotions. Feel them, but contain them."

– October 19, 2004

During the evening of October 20, 2004, after about ten days, I was officially discharged from the inpatient program. I was given a physical examination and proved to be in good health. Mentally, my doctor diagnosed my condition as "satisfactory and improved since admission." He said that I "participated actively in the group therapy classes" and that I said I felt like I gained a lot from the classes.

"Towards the end of her hospitalization, she came to see that the cancellation of the wedding was a blessing in disguise, especially in view of the fact that she only knew her fiancé for about nine or ten months prior to the wedding," he wrote. "Although she was feeling somewhat better by the end of her hospitalization, we felt that continued intensive therapy in the Partial Hospitalization Program would be beneficial and she was to start that program shortly after her discharge from inpatient."

Ten days may not sound like enough time to make progress toward mental healing, but when every day is filled from morning to night with little down time, you learn more about yourself than you ever knew before. You have constant activities consistently addressing your personal emotions and feelings, from conversing with professionals to literally writing down every sentiment bubbling inside you in a journal at the end of the day. For some patients, ten days is not enough. For others, it's more than enough. A lot of it, of course, depends on your condition coming in, but also on your attitude once you are there and how hard you work toward getting better.

Among the many things I learned, three aspects really stuck with me:

- I needed to have structure in my life every day to stay focused on my goals, with little down time to worry about those things that I could not change.
- The coping tools I learned were going to be my lifeline. With them, I could continually release an avalanche of emotions and live a normal life, even flourish. Without them, I would end up right back in the hospital.
- Mental illness is serious stuff and likely affects every family in some way, whether every family knows it or not.

Before I was admitted into South Coast, I was ignorant about mental illness, even though I had it. I had the same stereotypes toward it that others do, and I was as responsible as anyone for contributing to the stigma attached to it. I knew nothing about schizophrenia. I knew nothing about bipolar disorder. I quickly learned firsthand how mental illness affects everyday people who look and feel "normal." During my stay in South Coast, there was a woman who seemed to think she was a famous princess on one day, then somebody completely different the next day. There were women who were cutters (people who physically cut themselves in an attempt to release emotional pain), a problem that seems even more prevalent today, especially among teens.

Many of the patients had already tried to kill themselves, some multiple times. One male patient, a nineteen year old, walked the entire floor nonstop every day. After a day or two, a few other patients joined him. Then a few more. Eventually, it seemed like everybody was following him. It reminded me of the movie *Forrest Gump*, in which Forrest decided to start running just to run, and eventually people started to follow him. One day I stopped the guy and asked why he did that. He said it helped him clear his head and keep his mind off things.

What I witnessed with respect to some of my fellow patients often left me feeling sad. I knew that many of them would suffer for the rest of their lives, no matter how much treatment they received. It made my problems seem much less severe. I was battling, but not like they were. Their situations didn't minimize mine, but put mine in a better perspective for me. It helped strengthen my mind-set that I could do this, that I could overcome this.

My newfound awareness of how mentally ill people can be made me very proud of every single person who suffers from any form of mental illness and who takes action to try to get better. It also made me proud of those who have a hand in attempting to help those who are suffering.

Chapter 20

I Had to Earn It

"Why am I attending PHP? Because I need it. I need the classes, I need the therapists, I need to change. It is making me see that I need to make my own life and not rely on others to rescue me anymore. It is assisting me at looking at my own faults in my communication skills, life skills, coping skills, anger management, and expression. It is holding me accountable and empowering me every day, such as today when I was so tired and ready to not go, but knew I would miss out on good information that would only help me get better."

– October 22, 2004

With a successful ten days at South Coast, I felt ready for the outpatient program. I would attend every weekday from about 9 A.M. until 3 P.M. through the end of December 2004. The days would continue to be packed with classes and activities. The primary differences were that I would have to get myself there and home each day, and I would be forced to utilize everything I learned at the hospital in the real world, specifically in my chaotic home environment. It was time to stop talking and to start doing.

I never expected PHP to be easy, but I also never expected it to be as difficult as it was. The triggers when I was in inpatient were limited because I was in an isolated environment. But once I left, it was like leaving a sanitary bubble and entering an unsanitary world where anything could attack me at any time. Triggers lingered everywhere, from as minor as driving behind people who went fifteen miles below the speed limit to as large as my own family still not understanding my issues. I wasn't fully prepared for any of that yet.

> *"I came home from the hospital yesterday. I was anxious and nervous to be in the house. I went back to Sean's room to apologize to him because I was embarrassed for my actions and things I said about him on October 9, but he said he didn't have time for me. I just walked away and crossed my arms. I then walked back in the kitchen and slammed a door and screamed. 'This is the stuff I can't handle!' I yelled at my mom.*
>
> *"I sat on my bed and cried, asking myself why I am here. I took my pills, went to sleep, then woke up this morning to Denise screaming. Kato was dead* (Kato was Nicole's dog that she got for Sydney and Justin. Yes, they named him after Kato Kaelin, a witness in the trial. Kato was good friends with Nicole and the kids loved him). *It was the same thing ten years ago, but this time it was Kato instead of Nicole. I had to go to my first day of PHP before the doctor took Kato away. I said my good-byes to him, then went to the hospital in tears."*
>
> – October 21, 2004

What a start. My first day home and I have to immediately experience death again. Sure, it was a dog and not my sister or best friend, but whether you have ever had a pet or not, you know how much pets are part of the family. Kato's death was crushing. The worst part for me was that it was another chapter of Nicole's life that was gone. It was not what I needed to start PHP.

On top of that, and more importantly in the grand scheme of life, Sean rejected my desire to apologize to him. Many months would pass before he would give me the time of day. The lesson I learned from his rejection was that even though I felt like I was on the right track toward good mental health, it didn't automatically wash away my past transgressions in the eyes of those I hurt. Heck, Denise hadn't even visited me in the hospital and had no desire to talk to me when I was released. Forgiveness was going to have to be more than just saying I was sorry when *I* was ready to say it. I had to earn it over time by showing that I was a changed person.

But I was struggling big time.

> *"I came home from the hospital and just sat around, getting anxious, nervous, irritable, depressed. I isolated myself to my room. I took a nap. These classes do make me tired. I was cranky. I then got mad at myself for pondering it all. Why is it so difficult for me to just get out of bed and take a brisk walk or stretch, breathe, journal, do my worksheets? I sometimes get so paralyzed. Is this because of depression or laziness? I have no idea anymore. I want to change this about me. I have to stop being so passive in life."*
>
> *– October 25, 2004*

The reason for my struggles in PHP was obvious to me but not an easy short-term fix. I was simply not prepared to handle all of the triggers stinging me. I'm sure nobody at South Coast expected me to be fully ready since PHP was where I was really learning the dynamics of the coping tools. But I was supposed to apply what I learned each day in PHP at home, and it wasn't as black and white as I thought it would be. The triggers around me – my family members – had no sympathy. They hadn't gone through my classes with me. To them, Tanya was gone for ten days and was supposed to be better when she arrived home. Nobody said anything to them about me still being a major work in progress, or maybe treating me with kid gloves for a while. Their lives were still the same. This wasn't a fifty/fifty deal. I had to be the one to adjust 100 percent. I was the one with the problems, so I was the one who had to change, not them.

I used the private sessions in PHP to vent the frustrations I was facing at home, similar to the way I used them in inpatient. The group sessions were a different story. While I freely spoke in inpatient group therapy, I was initially reluctant to tell anybody my story in outpatient group. Maybe it's because it was a new group of people I didn't know. Maybe it's because of what happened at home with Sean and Kato those first two days home. Whatever the case, PHP was a daily challenge.

During much of PHP, I felt that any time I took one step forward through my classes, group therapy, individual therapy, or worksheets, I came home and took two steps backward. The tools I was learning about seemed effective as I was learning them by day, but they were not easy to apply at night. I would go to PHP, learn some new things, then come home and become frustrated with everybody. I would then go to PHP the next day and air those frustrations. That would make me feel better, but it was short-lived. I'd learn some new things, go home, and the vicious cycle would continue. I went to bed almost every night angry and aggravated.

Here are a few journal entries from that period to give you an idea of my difficulties:

> *"Well, yesterday and last night were not good for me. I pretty much slept all day. I woke up, cut my toe nails, picked my face, put on a mask, showered. Then went through my boxes that my ex packed for me. Every time I spoke of him, to him, or about him in the hospital, it set me back to those ten days of hell (when he broke the engagement). That is why I have opted to close the door on him. But I still feel suffocated. I just wish there could be silence. No speaking, no dishes clanking, no loud yelling, no dogs barking. I just wish."*

> *– November 14, 2004*

> *"The first group activity of the day was on creative restructuring and we were playing a Pictionary game with mottos, such as 'an apple a day keeps the doctor away.' There were too many people in the room, first of all, to play the game. Second, it was too loud. People playing over each other. I am sitting there feeling anxious and stressed out to the max. Someone saying 'You go TB, come on.' I kept saying no because I can feel the tension rising. But I gave in and drew a card: 'You can't unscramble your eggs.' Meaning? You can't change your past. Hmmm! Then I sat down and the game*

continued. I was getting more and more agitated, irritated, all of the verbs.

"At the end, my occupational therapist and her coworker asked 'What did you get from this game?' I exploded! This game stressed me out. There was too much chaos, too many voices, people talking too loud. All of a sudden the boiling pot ran over. I popped. Two other patients there wanted to console me. I told them, 'Don't touch me!'"

– December 9, 2004

"Well good &*#%*$@ morning! I thought yesterday and the last couple of days were going well. In fact, they were going awesome. But this morning I knew this down would come. I knew it. Every &*#%*$@ time that I am too happy I always fall down. I made a joke and Mom told me not to say it in front of others. Man, this is a perfect example! Every time I say something it is always followed by a comment from someone. Can't I just say something and not hear about it?! Denise says &#*% like that all the time and nobody says anything, but they do it to me all the time. So I said I am not going to speak anymore. I am just going to shut up."

– December 18, 2004

You can see the dates on those entries, spread out over the course of my PHP, which ended on December 30. So was I actually getting better if I was still in a rage on December 18? I know it doesn't sound like it, but believe it or not, I was better, because I continued to learn those coping tools as I went along. It's just that, as in many situations in life, the negative can often overshadow the positive until you have ultimately achieved your goal.

A huge breakthrough came about a week into PHP when – with the help of fellow patient and friend Kate Hughes, a woman I'd confided in earlier in the week with my story – I finally told my tale in our group session. It was long and emotional. My nose was running and my eyes were dripping with tears as I sent the hospital's tissue budget skyrocketing. I rambled for most of the class, but I let it all out, from Herissa to Nicole to Troy to my ex. While I would have many more rough days ahead, that release helped me to push forward ... to want to push forward. And the group's receptiveness – it was easy to forget that they all had their own issues, some worse than mine – made it that much easier.

Here is one way to look at what I was going through in PHP. Let's say you want to play soccer but aren't very good at it. So each day you are taught by a pro how to do certain drills and moves, but then each of those nights you are thrown into real games against skilled opponents who have no sympathy for the fact that you are new to the game. Frustrating? Of course. But you keep practicing and learning more as the days go on. You continue to play a game each night and continue to get your butt kicked and continue to get frustrated, but you are also getting better in the process. That's what this was like for me. I received my training by day, but then had a real game situation each night at home where my triggers were waiting to set me off. Sure, I had plenty of setbacks. I wondered sometimes if I would make it. But here was the key:

I never considered quitting.

It was a painful process, but I was determined to do it. I knew where I'd been, and I didn't want to go back to that place. I didn't want to be that person I once was. I needed to change. I did not want to walk out of South Coast as the same Tanya Brown I was two months earlier.

And I didn't.

I learned the coping tools and had them firmly planted in my mind when I was discharged on December 30. I adapted them to my own life and called them *Tanya's Tools for Change*. Next was the implementation, and I was on my own. The people at South Coast did a great job of carefully guiding me through the tools each day. Now I had to put them to use without my hand being held. Once I mastered that, I would be the new person I wanted to be.

CHAPTER 21

TOOL #1 – SCHEDULE IT!

Time management is life management

"Went over all of my notes from inpatient and reworked all of the points. I also made my schedule for the week. That felt good, because now I have goals and stuff I need to do. I know I am lucky to be here, and I want to use my time productively and efficiently, so time management is going to be big with me."

– October 25, 2004

(Note: This tool and the eleven tools that follow are in no particular order. Certain tools will be more valuable to you than others, depending upon your situation. Also, many of the titles of these tools were created by me, and may not be exactly what they were called at South Coast. The purpose of the concise titles I gave them, such as Schedule It! is to make them easy for you to remember and organize).

Ken D. Foster, author of *Ask and You Will Succeed*, said: "A calm and organized mind creates a calm and organized life." So simple, yet so true.

Scheduling, and sticking to that schedule, takes discipline and focus. We all have very busy lives, and there are always other things that we can be doing. But there comes a point (oftentimes more than once) in each day when we are at a crossroads, where we need to make a choice of what to do next.

How do we make that choice without becoming overwhelmed and stressed?

By having an organized life.

Time management is life management. Our time is our life. Yet time gets away from us all, sometimes barely a couple hours into our day. We wake up, go to work or school, tend to our children, prepare meals, run errands, attend meetings or other activities, do household chores, get ready for tomorrow. When we realize all the tasks we didn't complete by the end of the day, we are rattling off the old clichés of "Where did the day go?" or "There are only so many hours in a day."

What really helped me attain control of my days and eliminate a great deal of anxiety was creating a time management schedule. I'm not talking about just a general to-do list of the major things that need to be done each day. I'm talking about creating a daily and weekly calendar that budgets every moment of time down to the nitty-gritty details. It's not something you need to do for the rest of your life, but do it until you are in the habit of knowing how to prioritize and realizing how important every minute is.

Begin by creating a list of everything that needs to be done. And when I say create it, I mean write it down. If you try to keep everything in your head, you will undoubtedly forget something, and the list will likely overwhelm you at some point, which can lead to anxiety and depression.

Take the large tasks and break them down as much as you can so that you can complete them in small steps. It will help you establish priorities and set daily scheduling that is manageable and measurable. It will also help you identify those things you can do, delete, or delegate, which will take pressure off of you and ease potential frustration.

For example, don't write "Get ready for work in the morning." List everything involved in getting ready: making your bed, showering, brushing your teeth, curling your hair, eating breakfast. Don't forget to add in your driving time to work or school. I did that when I was in the outpatient program at South Coast, even though it was just five minutes away. Note how long each task should take, even if it's just two or three minutes, then pad each by a few minutes to give yourself some breathing room. Check off each item as you finish it, not only to keep yourself on schedule, but to give yourself a feeling of accomplishment. "Wow, it's 7 A.M. and I've already done six things!" Even if those things don't seem like much, they still had to be completed, and you accomplished that goal, so feel good about it.

While making your schedule, identify potential obstacles that can arise with each task, then identify ways they can be solved. For example, if you run into unexpected traffic, are there detours you can take? Also identify coping skills to help you emotionally push through those roadblocks. If there are no detours and you have to wait out the traffic, a couple of other tools, such as *Accept and Surrender!* or *Break Free!* may be ideal in helping you arrive at your destination a happy person.

At the end of each day, grade yourself on how well you accomplished each task and determine what you could do better the next time. Does one task need more time? Is there a task that can be eliminated, or maybe done the night before?

I know many people who live care-free lives who may think this tool is too restrictive. But as odd as this may sound, this tool can actually give you more freedom. If you create and stick to a schedule each day, your tasks will be completed in a more efficient manner, leaving you more free time to be spontaneous and do the things you want to do. There won't be any last-minute scrambling at the end of the day because "Oh, I forgot to do that" or "I still have three more things to do." Most importantly, the pressure that those situations can create in your mind won't exist.

I often speak on college campuses, and this *Schedule It!* tool is one I place at the top of the list for students. When I attended UC San Diego, it was a huge life-changing experience for me, as going away to college normally is for every student. Also, like many first-time college students, I was not the most organized person. I was used to living at home, having the things I needed there for me, or done for me by my parents. I always had backup. There was more structure in high school and at home. In college, I quickly learned I was on my own, and it overwhelmed me my very first day.

I got up that morning a little later than I should have and was scurrying to get ready for my first class. When I arrived there, I found it to be in a huge lecture hall with about four hundred students, more than ten times larger than any high school class I ever had. Of course, by the time I arrived there, the front row was all that was open. I sat down but was instantly overwhelmed as I became aware of my unfamiliar surroundings – the number of students, size of the room, being ninety minutes from home, doubts about whether I belonged there. Did I have the right books for class? What was I forgetting? Did I bring a pen? Where was my next class? What if I don't understand something in the lecture … was I really supposed to raise my hand in front of hundreds of other students I didn't know? In a matter of seconds I had talked myself into a panic attack. I jumped from my chair and ran out the door just as the professor was coming in. When I got outside the room, I was turning pale as I leaned my hand against a brick wall to support myself.

"Are you okay?" a couple of girls about to enter the class asked me. I remember telling them no, and that's all I remember because I fainted. When I finally awoke, I was lying on the floor and staring up at those same two girls, who were on their knees asking me again if I was okay. I sat up, then got to my feet and made a mad dash to the bathroom, where I threw up. Distressed and dehydrated, I ended up spending my first day in the health clinic. What a great start to my college career.

What was frustrating about that attack was that it was purely self-induced, and I can't help but think how that situation would have been reversed if I knew then what I know today about coping and structure. I had some structure in my life before heading to college, but it was all created by others, such as my school and parents, and not by me. I showed up as a small fish in a big ocean, having never lived away from home, facing a brand new experience, and in a huge city.

If I had gone in knowing about structure, about breathing techniques, about how to disengage from stress, I believe the experience would have been completely different. If you're graduating from high school and are about to leave home for the first time, or starting a new job, or making some other major change in your life, don't take it for granted that you will be able to ease into it. Physically, sure, you can get where you need to be. But mentally, it's a whole different ballgame. The stress is waiting to burst out. But with these coping tools, you can not only manage and survive your new experience, but thoroughly enjoy it.

CHAPTER 22

TOOL #2 – BE PRESENT!

Finding the calm within you

"What am I doing to support my commitment here? I am trying every day with every word that I speak to say it right. To say it clean and not with anger or anxiety. I am more aware than ever how true it is when they say: 'Say what you mean, mean what you say, and don't say it mean.'"

– October 29, 2004

Buddha was quoted as saying: "Do not dwell in the past, do not dream of the future, concentrate the mind on the present moment." How difficult is that? Extremely! We are always thinking about what was, what could have been, and what is going to happen tomorrow ... or even in the next five minutes. I just gave you a tool about planning out your day and week down to the minute. Isn't that dreaming of the future? Yes, it is. But that planning can also include time to be present.

I have found that the best way for me to be present is to schedule time each day for meditation. It can be for ten minutes, twenty minutes, longer – whatever time you can afford. I wrote earlier about meditation and about how it is not a religion, as some people think. It is a state of peace and deep relaxation. If you practice it, you will no doubt find everyday life to be much more serene. You will be able to approach difficult situations with patience, care, and acceptance.

After every long day at South Coast during my outpatient therapy, I drove to the beach before going home. I parked the car overlooking the ocean, rolled down the windows, put on my headphones, turned on the music that relaxed me most, pushed my seat back, and closed my eyes. Can I make it sound any more relaxing?

I recall one week in early 2013 when I had become horribly overwhelmed and anxious. I was closing in on the end of school and had to write my final paper. I was also planning a short trip to New York City with a friend to see her son's Off-Broadway play, and I was in the midst of writing my book. I couldn't escape the stress, and it seemed like everything and everyone around me had become a trigger. I was way over-stimulated. Finally, one afternoon, I just stopped.

I just stopped.

Think about that for a moment. All the noise. All the bedlam. All the people. And it's like you just flip a switch and it's all off, all gone. I did that by retreating to my bedroom, lying down on my bed, and listening to myself breathe. I did this for about an hour without falling asleep, visualizing myself alone with nothing but the peaceful sounds of nature in my mind. Just that little bit of a break calmed me down and helped me regain some control over my life. The batteries were recharged, and I was ready to continue forward.

Being present and finding the calm within you can also happen with others present; it does not always involve isolating yourself from the world.

For example, my mom and I take walks almost daily with our dog, Winston. It's a chance for us to have some quiet time and enjoy each other's company. Of course, I often find myself spending that time going against Buddha's advice and talking to her about what I did that day, or what I have to do tomorrow. Mom, on the other hand, has become a master at being present. Almost inevitably, on every walk we take, she stops in her tracks to point out how beautiful the colors are on a flower petal along the path. It's the smallest of things, but something I envy about her. She has never taken any courses on coping skills or being present. She's just that way. When we are present, we are able to see and appreciate the beauty, the natural beauty, that surrounds us. But rarely do any of us take that time to stop and smell the roses … literally, as Mom does!

Another example of being present with others happened one day after my yoga class. It was a great session, leaving me feeling more relaxed than I had been in a while. On my way out I walked by the instructor, who was in the midst of a conversation with another student. I placed my hand on her shoulder.

"Great class today!" I said to her enthusiastically.

She barely looked at me, never acknowledging the compliment and continuing her conversation with the other person. She was normally very nice. It wasn't like her to brush me off, and I was a bit bothered by what I perceived as her rudeness. A simple "thank you" would have been nice.

About a week had gone by when I was reading some literature on the topic of "enlightenment." It pointed out that when we are in a state of such intense presence, we are completely enlightened, so enlightened that we don't see or hear anything outside of the subject we are focused on at that moment. In a sense, we have become one with that subject. It's like meditating in public. That's when it clicked with me. That yoga instructor wasn't being rude. In fact, I was the one being rude by trying to interrupt her conversation. She was just completely engrossed in the present, completely engaged with that other person. It was such a beautiful awakening for me.

To be present is definitely a skill. It usually takes mindful practice and sometimes, as ironic as it sounds, a little pre-planning. Plan your meditations each day, Plan to turn off all technology at some point in the day and enjoy the earth. Plan your time of peace. Once you commit to it and get good at it, you will definitely find the calm within you.

CHAPTER 23

TOOL #3 – BREAK FREE!

Disengage from the triggers, stress, and chaos

"I had such a wonderful evening last night. I relaxed, watched TV, and hung out with my friend, Ashley. I really appreciate these quiet times. I am going to relinquish my insecurities, hesitations, skepticism, and all other negative thought patterns. I intend to live my life with the desire to make other's lives enjoyable and meaningful."

– March 17, 2005

Have you ever seen the movie *Silver Linings Playbook*? In a therapy session, the doctor told Bradley Cooper's character, Pat, to get control of his feelings and calm down. Pat said it was easier said than done, but the doctor told him that he still must try to do it. I agree that many things are easier said than done, but the truth is whatever it is that has to be done *can* be done if you have the support and tools.

When someone makes you angry, or if you are about to yell at your child for tracking mud into the house, or if you want to throw something across the room because of a bad situation at work, just walk away, take a deep breath, and count to five. Maybe ten. Maybe twenty. Whatever feels right. Then come back and revisit the situation.

I talked about the stress that the presence of my ex-fiancé put me under when I was at South Coast. He came to visit me on several occasions but, as much as I appreciated it, my blood boiled every time he came because of how our engagement ended. I tried counting to five every time he was there, but it didn't work. My "count to five" finally became taking him off my visitors list, and a huge chunk of my stress immediately dissipated.

The night I flipped out on my family, I had to disengage myself from my environment to calm myself down. I had to get control of my emotions and breathing. I had to get as far away from them as possible. As far away from the wine and pills as possible. I needed a change of scenery, a change in my routine. I needed a safe place where I could calm down and be away from all the chaos. We all feel stress, and oftentimes we can easily manage that stress. But sometimes we can't. That's when we need to take a break from it, before it consumes us and becomes very unhealthy or even dangerous.

Beginning in the late 2000s and into the early 2010s, my life had become consumed with chaos at home. I was going to graduate school, was working on this book, and was trying to promote my speaking and coaching business. At the same time, my living environment was anything but ideal. Mom had just been diagnosed with stage 3C breast cancer and had lymph nodes removed, while my dad's dementia was getting worse and growing into full-blown Alzheimer's disease. Mini and her son were also living there. I needed and wanted to be there for Mom and Dad, but the living arrangement was stressful. It was crowded. Noisy. People were constantly coming and going. Triggers of overstimulation were everywhere all the time.

So how did I cope with it?

I created a space in the back of our house where I did my homework, worked on my speaking and coaching business, and wrote my book. I set aside specific times to work on all of that and specific times to come out and help my mom with Dad, giving her some space and time to herself that she so desperately needed. Selfishly, I say, it wasn't easy for me. Sometimes I felt transported back to when I snapped in 2004. But I did what had to be done.

Today, with Mom in her eighties and Dad in poor health, I still live at home to help them as much as I can. So what do I do if the noise and commotion get to be too much for me? First, I usually get frustrated, something that will never go away; that just comes with being human and being Tanya. But how I react to that frustration is the difference. Instead of screaming or yelling or getting all flustered, I ask one of my sisters or my nephew for help with my parents. Or I retreat to my bedroom for a while if it's just noise I'm trying to avoid. Notice that this situation isn't any different than in 2004. Loud noises, lots of people, lots of chaos. The difference is in how I handle it, by applying the *Break Free!* tool.

Here's another story:

I had to transcribe a counseling session for one of the classes I was taking in graduate school. It was a tedious assignment that involved filling out columns and typing verbatim conversations, including client responses and/or better options to the client responses. Sound boring? Imagine having to listen to it all, then having to listen to it all again in order to transcribe it. I had such a bad attitude that day because of the nature of the project.

When I arrived home from school, I immediately jumped on it to get it out of the way. My family knew that I had to complete it, and they were even willing to help me out. Mini set up the spreadsheet that I needed because she knew how much computers and technology stressed me out. While she was doing that, my dad was hovering over us having a nonsensical conversation. He can still walk and talk, and he looks great, but his Alzheimer's causes him to ramble a lot, especially at the end of the day; this syndrome is known as Sundowners. Normally I can deal with it pretty well, but given the stress I was feeling because of the project, his presence was only adding more stress. After Mini set up the spreadsheet and left the room so I could get to work, Dad stayed, continuing to linger over my shoulder and talk and talk and talk. Dad was my trigger, and I was becoming extremely agitated inside. My blood was at a boiling point. But after recognizing and feeling the emotions he was triggering in me, I accepted them.

OK, I thought to myself while taking a deep breath. *Daddy is here, so there is no sense in trying to plow through the stress. I am only going to get angrier and not do a good job on this project, which will only snowball my anger.* On top of that, and most importantly, he was my dad, for goodness sake! Sometimes stress can be so overwhelming that it can overshadow the love and goodness inside of us. I realized that I not only needed to disengage, but I also needed to be present for my dad.

With that, I closed the laptop, smiled at Dad, and walked him into the living room where we sat down and talked with each other until he was too tired to talk any longer. Once he was quiet and relaxed, I went back to the dining room table and began working on my project. I had been stuck in the frustration he was causing me rather than trying to figure out how to disengage from it. All it took was closing my laptop and walking away. Pretty easy. The time I spent with him in the living room was not only some quality time for us, but it was time not spent getting angry at him while trying to work on my project.

Triggers will never go away, but there are always ways to disengage them. Identify who and what drains you. Break these triggers into sections: family, environment, the workplace. You will probably find that you put up with, accept, take on, allow, and are dragged down by people's behaviors, situations, unmet needs, crossed boundaries, frustrations, and problems much more than you think you do.

Figure out what is draining your energy and write it down. Do you have to actually do anything about it? Maybe. It depends on the situation. Maybe there is somebody you need to confront about something, or somebody you need to cut out of your life. Or you may find that you don't need to do anything in particular except become aware of those people and things and articulate them to yourself to bring them to the forefront of your soul. That's when you will naturally start breaking free.

CHAPTER 24

TOOL #4 – EXPRESS IT!

Be toxic-free

"My goal for tomorrow is to take advantage of my quiet times and journaling. I know this is what will heal me. This is what will help me grow, figure out who I am, where I want to go, and how I am going to get there."

– October 12, 2004

When we don't express our feelings, especially for a long length of time, we become toxic. We poison ourselves. We decrease our longevity, joy, and happiness, and we begin to resent everyone and everything around us. That eventually begins to affect our physical health as well. I'm proof of all that.

The bottom line is this: do not ignore how you feel. When I ignored my feelings and kept them stuffed inside, I eventually exploded and nearly took my own life. Talk about your problems to your friends, your family, a mental health professional, a minister, even to yourself through journaling. Don't hide what you feel. Don't try to fool yourself. Don't try to be macho and think that you can handle what is going on inside you all by yourself without expressing yourself. Maybe you can to an extent, but as I said in the very first line of this book, each of us has a mental breaking point.

Be authentic with yourself and others. Time heals wounds, but not on its own. Time and talking are, together, what heal wounds. That combination is how my relationship with Denise healed. I can't say, nor can she, that there was one defining moment in our relationship in which things suddenly became better between us. It was a combination of several things: me getting help, her seeing that I was seeking help, her learning about depression, me seeing that she was learning about depression, us having conversations with each other about anything rather than trying to avoid each other. I'd be willing to bet that she expressed herself by talking to other people about her frustrations with me. And, speaking for myself, I wrote a great deal about her in my journal and expressed my feelings about her to my therapists. Much of it was negative, especially early on. But the more I wrote and talked, the more placid I became. The more I expressed myself, the more I learned about myself and Denise, and eventually, with time, all was well between us.

I've talked a lot about the power of journaling and hopefully by now, having read many of my entries, you have a sense of just how powerful it can be. Journaling was a primary self-care tool that helped me then and continues to help me today. It did not start off easy, though. Facing my anger, the darkness, and the losses I never coped with by writing them out was initially very difficult. At times it didn't even make sense to me to do it because of all the negative thoughts I had. So why would I do that to myself? I was reliving day after day after day all of the pain I had gone through the previous fifteen years. But I learned it was a great way to vent my frustrations and to analyze what I was feeling. It helped me to figure out that a situation that occurred on a particular day wasn't as bad as I initially thought. It gave me an opportunity to express the good things that happened and to see the positives occurring in my life. All this can be difficult to recognize when you are suffering with depression.

I still journal today and always will. I've even reached a point where I journal so much that, as I go through my day and something interesting happens, good or bad, I tell myself I need to journal it later. If it's a bad thing, I know that since I will be revisiting it later in a calm environment, I don't need to fret over it at the moment. If it's a good thing I'm going to write, it makes me happy to know I will be reliving that moment later in my mind.

In 2013, when I was working on my book, my co-author came into town to meet my family and see various sites. We went to Nicole's grave, to the mortuary where she had been laid out, to the church where the funeral had been held, to Bundy, to Rockingham, to Mission (formerly South Coast). While it was an information-gathering trip for him, it was an emotional, but healthy, experience for me. I hadn't been to many of those places since Nicole died. While there was some pain seeing it all again, it was an opportunity for me to reminisce about Nicole and to realize how far I'd come emotionally in nearly twenty years. All day I kept saying "I can't wait to journal this! I can't wait to journal that!" When you make your daily schedule, include time at the end of the day for journaling if you can. It will be some of your best time spent each day.

While journaling is a very simple process, a quick Internet search can lead you to dozens of tips that can help you get started and journal more effectively. Here are ten tips I learned at South Coast to keep in mind as I journal:

1) *Write every day. Record everything, from your thoughts and feelings to your daydreams. What you write is not as initially important as simply getting into the habit of writing something each day.*

2) *Write in the first person. Be present when you write!*

3) *Write as you think – in phrases, fragments, poetry, good language, bad language, whatever. Don't change who you are. You are writing this for yourself, not for someone else (unless you eventually write a book like I did, but it was my choice to share what I wrote).*

4) *Do not worry about spelling or grammar.*

5) *Do not erase what you write. Go with your first thoughts, and just add to them if necessary.*

6) *Write quickly as you are thinking. There should be some spontaneity to it.*

7) *The more you journal, the better you will be at it.*

8) *Write the way you naturally write or talk.*

9) *For some people, journaling is easier if they write as if they are talking to a specific person – a friend, relative, counselor, etc.*

10) *There is no wrong way to journal. Your way is the right way. Trust yourself and your inner voice.*

Another tip I have learned on my own that has worked well for me is to use a pen and paper rather than a computer. While a computer is certainly more efficient in many ways, I have found that there are too many potential distractions. If I don't want to be journaling, then I pause for a moment to check email or a social media site or play a quick game of solitaire. Journaling should be a time when you can fully reflect upon your day, upon your feelings, and express them in the most honest way possible without any interruptions.

Finally, while there is no wrong way to journal, (as stated in tip No. 10), one technique I did learn at South Coast that can really help in the journaling process is to *Give Gratitude!* each time you journal. That taught me two things: that journaling doesn't have to be negative, and that I have a lot in my life that I need to appreciate.

Journaling does not always have to be filled with hostility or sadness. I was good at writing the negative thoughts. Many people are because those are the kinds of thoughts you want to clear from your head at the end of the day. But emphasizing the positives is equally important. When you do so, you can better see the goodness in your life. I had so much negativity in my life, so much taken away from me, that I couldn't always see the wonderful things right in front of me. Writing it on paper was a way to acknowledge it all and help me realize that despite my problems, I was, in many respects, one very lucky gal.

CHAPTER 25

TOOL #5 – GIVE GRATITUDE!

Five things a day to keep the doctor at bay

"Today I begin with a new perspective to journaling. Along with venting my frustrations and struggles, I am also going to add my gratitude towards and for my life. I see clearly now. I was unable to see clearly how beautiful life was. I now can see what is healthy for me and what is not. Now, today, I really get it."

– March 14, 2005

If you recall in the letter I wrote to my parents recorded in Chapter 5, I gave gratitude for the things I was thankful for that day, such as seeing a butterfly and receiving an unexpected compliment. *Give Gratitude!* journaling is very simple: you list five things (or more if you'd like) that you are grateful for, usually at the end of your journaling each day so you can close your journal on a positive note. The listed items don't have to include anything big. In fact, recognizing some of the smaller things can often open your eyes to the beautiful world around you, like Mom stopping to look at the flowers on our walks.

The best way for me to explain this to you is to give a few examples from my journals:

"I am feeling nervous right now. I just got done with cleaning my room. It was either that or go to bed. God, what is this? Why do I have such a terrible internal battle going

on when it comes to making decisions of any kind? I guess I am still vulnerable. But let me tell you, Lord, what I was grateful for today:

- *The opportunity to speak to a social worker here.*
- *The opportunity to get to know one of the other patients.*
- *Getting my feelings out about Nicole's murder.*
- *My dog.*
- *The outing with my mom.*
- *My dog welcoming me home.*
- *Being able to drive in public without worry. I was calm and didn't wig out.*
- *Being hospitalized so I could learn to be a better person."*

– October 25, 2004

As you can see, some of those were very broad comments, such as being grateful that I was in the hospital and that I was able to speak to a social worker. Then there were the smaller items, such as my dog welcoming me home, and me being able to drive without freaking out. Writing each of those things made me feel better about myself, gave me a sense that I was making progress in my therapy, and helped me appreciate all that I had. I didn't focus on what I didn't have.

Here is another example of giving gratitude.

"I am so happy and grateful for:

- *Going back to school. I will have completed my B.A. soon, and I am so excited and proud of myself for really realizing that I wanted to simplify my life. I want to get a job as an occupational therapist in a hospital and help people move forward in their lives. It's not a lot of money, but I will enjoy it and help people along the way.*
- *Having the ambition to go beyond my B.A. and get two master's degrees, one in counseling and one in occupational therapy. I am just going to apply for loans. I want to make my life as simple as possible.*

- *Having a roof over my head. Although it's not what I really want (to live with my folks), I am grateful I can stay here, go to school, and then get a job somewhere and live on my own.*

- *Self-sufficiency. This is a new concept for me. My entire life (other than my UCSD days) I have always relied on others. I have learned that I am a woman with so much to give, offer, and love that I am going to rely on me.*

- *I am really grateful God, and I am so excited about this new, improved, and more focused life. I feel great. Thank you!"*

– April 24, 2005

Looking at that entry also gave me a glimpse into how my goals changed over the years. I planned to get two master's degrees. I ended up getting one in Counseling Psychology, and believe me, that was enough considering all the work it took. I had planned to be an occupational therapist. I am a full-time speaker and author instead. No, I may not have done exactly what I said I would professionally, but that's normal. We all change our minds for various reasons as the years go on. But what gratitude journaling did for me back then was help me set and stay on a path of happiness. I have no regrets whatsoever for not getting a second master's, or not being an occupational therapist. I love what I do. I am happy. And I give gratitude for that every day.

Chapter 26

Tool #6 – Praise Yourself!

Every little step counts

"My heart is abundantly pure. Sort of. It means well. My intention in life is to serve others, to embrace and appreciate people's differences and similarities. I am going to put a stop to my negative comments about myself and others. From this day forward I will have a pure heart with pure intentions."

– March 14, 2005

Love who you are and make the changes in your life that you want to make, not that someone else wants you to make. Accomplish those changes without them being a chore – changes should be part of your journey toward happiness – and praise yourself each step of the way.

When I went back to college to get my master's degree, I was so incredibly hard on myself if I didn't get an A in a class. One semester I had to take Advanced Counseling Theories. It was as difficult as it sounds, and I not only let it consume me, but I let the thought of getting anything less than an A stress the heck out of me. The day of one of our biggest exams was my birthday. I worried about that test for weeks, never enjoyed my birthday for a second, and burst into tears when the test was over because of all the stress that had built inside of me. That emotional release made me realize everything I had put myself through mentally during those weeks prior wasn't worth it. Yes, I needed to give full effort, but the grade I got did not change all the hard work I'd put into that class. I needed to learn to strive for progress, not perfection. If I earned a B or B minus, it wasn't the end of the world. And in the end, that's what I got … a B. And I was fine with that. And everything was good. And I moved on and continued with the pursuit of my degree.

You don't need to praise yourself publicly. Just quietly give yourself a pat on the back when you know you've done something the right way. It requires a little bit of ego, but we all need to have a little bit of an ego to be mentally healthy. As angry as I was some days at South Coast, I tried to remember to praise myself daily in my journals for not quitting, for wanting to get through the treatment, for wanting to be a better person. They were small praises that nobody else probably thought about giving me, but articulating them meant everything to me and helped me keep going. I even praised myself some days just for getting out of bed, which wasn't always easy. It may sound trivial, but sometimes getting out of bed was a major step for me, as many who suffer with depression can attest to.

There were countless times in the outpatient program when I was very emotional and, of course, it didn't take much at home to make me upset. My routine included slamming doors, screaming at somebody, crying. I struggled to contain my emotions once they were triggered. But as time would pass and I would calm down and reflect on my actions, I'd realize all the good things I did that day and would give myself a little credit. It's much like someone in Alcoholics Anonymous. I'd realize that I just had to take it day by day and cherish the small victories I had achieved.

There is always something you can learn about yourself through your struggles, even if it is a small self-awareness. Ask yourself: "What did I learn about myself today, yesterday, or this past week?" If you can be aware of thoughts, behaviors, or feelings that you learned, praise yourself because it means you are growing as a person.

Just prior to my breakdown, I had signed a contract to speak at a battered women's shelter in Alaska about domestic violence. Little did I know, of course, that my breakdown was about to happen. The date of the talk was scheduled for early December, during the same time as my eventual outpatient treatment at South Coast. Obviously, once I started treatment, I assumed there was no way I was going to be in the right frame of mind to participate in such an event. But I signed a contract and had never backed out of one before. I felt that canceling a speaking engagement for the first time would be a major setback, so I arranged to take a couple of days off from therapy to make the trip.

I gave two talks. One was a short, private presentation for people at the shelter. The other was for a larger crowd of maybe a couple hundred people associated with the shelter. Those were the most difficult talks I ever had to give for two reasons: I had the worst cold in the world and was feeling physically awful, and I was not in the best state psychologically. How many people leave a psych unit to give a presentation and speech in front of other people?

I was absolutely miserable during the speech to the larger crowd. My nose was red and running. My eyes were watering. At one point, someone from the audience came up and handed me a box of tissues. I can't even imagine what I looked like, but I plowed through it the best I could. I also brought some drama to the private presentation I gave. It was held in a conference room with large windows and a view of the glorious mountains. As I was in the midst of speaking, fighting through my cold, I lost focus of my audience and was overwhelmed by the beauty of the mountains behind them. So much so that I broke down and cried. Or, as I later wrote in my journal, I "exploded."

> *"The mountains were incredible, Alaska truly was so majestic. Never saw anything like it. The speech went fantastic. People were so intrigued by Nicole's story and by our family's dilemmas and my personal one about depression. I finally exploded. In other words, I got real with them. I got real with myself."*
>
> – December 6, 2004

At first I was ashamed and embarrassed I had let those emotions out, but the people at the shelter were generous with their support. After returning home and returning to therapy, I learned more about the *Praise Yourself!* tool. I was proud of myself for expressing such an emotion that warmed my spirit. Today, Alaska is my "happy place" I revert to in my mind during times of distress.

What I learned about myself after the Alaska trip was that I had been excited about going on it, but then just hit a brick wall that afternoon as my emotions became too much to handle. Imagine giving a talk in front of strangers about domestic violence and what your dead sister suffered, all while you are in the midst of going through therapy yourself, and sick with a cold on top of that. Not an easy task. I was so emotionally wiped out. I learned how sensitive and fragile I was, and how easily my mood could be triggered by anything and in front of anyone.

I could have decided I was finished speaking for good after that experience, or I could have quit therapy because it didn't appear, on the surface, that it was working. How could I say it was working when I cried in front of all those people? But I chose, instead, to see the good that came from the trip and the many things I learned about myself. Instead of focusing on my breakdown during the talk and how negative that could have appeared to some people, I praised myself for going forward with my obligation to speak and for the positive effect I may have had on those women.

What I did at that delicate moment in my life took a lot of courage, strength, will, and passion. Sound a little self-centered? Sure, but that's okay. Don't ever hesitate to praise yourself for your hard work, no matter how insignificant it may feel. It matters. You matter! Praise yourself for your accomplishments, especially when you're under stress.

CHAPTER 27

TOOL #7 – IDENTIFY AND MANAGE YOUR THOUGHTS!

Convince yourself that you can do it

"I have learned a lot about myself this past year. I look back and realize that I was out of sync. That is why life was so difficult for me. But, it was through my recent face with emotional trauma that I embraced my newfound life and will now live each day with intention."

– March 16, 2005

Pay attention to all of your negative thoughts. Every one of them. You know, those voices that say you can't do this or you can't do that or you aren't smart enough or your dreams will never come true. Listen to them … and then destroy them with positive affirmations.

In therapy I did a *Daily Mood Log* that was created by renowned clinical psychiatrist Dr. David D. Burns. The purpose of it was to teach us how to turn negative thoughts into positive ones, like the old saying of turning lemons into lemonade. One of the thoughts I wrote down about myself was, "I am so discouraged that nothing is working out for me." The mood log helps you identify how much of that statement is actually true. I, of course, thought it was completely true. I thought nothing was working for me. But when we did a group assessment and the group shared what positive qualities they saw in me, I was able to turn around my negativity and say, "I believe in myself, and I am no longer discouraged."

When we are stuck in such a negative mind-set, it is critical to immediately start to try to turn it around. My mom continually did that for me after Herissa died. When I wasn't eating, remember those affirmations she posted around the house about what a great person I was? No, the affirmations didn't work on the spot because I was so deep into depression. But we have to start somewhere, and I did eventually reflect upon them when I realized I needed to change. Trying to find the positives in every situation is always a great starting point toward turning it around.

I have learned the best way to reprogram negative thoughts into positive thoughts is to simply repeat affirmations. The two most powerful words known to mankind are "I am." I am loved, I am healthy, I am lucky, I am beautiful, I am successful. "I am" has the power to change your life. You can find several tips in books and on the Internet for creating affirmations. Here are six I learned at South Coast:

1) *Always use the present tense, as if it already exists (even if it doesn't). For example, "I am strong" or "I have a wonderful family."*

2) *Use only positive words; avoid negative ones.*

3) *Speak your affirmations using first person.*

4) *Each affirmation should create a strong, successful vision of you.*

5) *Keep it short and to the point.*

6) *If you have faith in a higher power, use it to enhance your affirmations.*

Here are some examples of affirmations South Coast gave me: I think and act with confidence; I am strong and powerful; I have many accomplishments to my credit; I deserve the time and space to heal; I am safe and protected; I am effective and efficient in stressful situations; I look and feel wonderful; I am a very valuable person; and I am in charge of my life.

Once you have created your affirmations, repeat and re-peat and repeat them some more throughout the day, especial-ly when you start getting that sinking feeling that you are go-ing to turn negative about something. You will be amazed how your thoughts will become reality when you hone this skill.

Feeling and visualizing your affirmations is another great skill to develop. When reviewing one of my journals eight years later, I noticed this little nugget:

> *"I intend to invest in someone to help me write my book. This is what I want to do with my life. I want to have my words flow so that they will help people, so that people will be inspired by them, so that they will be a life-saving tool. I see people enjoying reading it, and I see myself enjoying the success and happiness it is bringing to me."*
>
> – March 17, 2005

I'd been telling myself for years I wanted to write an in-spirational book about everything I'd been through. School or work or something else going on in my life always stood in the way of me doing it, but none of that ever stopped me from continuing to say I wanted to write it. And by repeatedly visu-alizing it over the years, it finally happened. I don't believe it ever would have if I had not had that visualization or feeling it would one day come to fruition.

Having inner dialogue churning is common for me, but it hasn't always been kind dialogue. When I was in the hospital, some of my most common daily lines were: I hate myself; I shouldn't have to be here; I suck; I'm a horrible person; this is all so hard; my family should be able to understand what I'm going through. Then I learned about positive affirmations and changed those phrases to: I love myself; I am here to get healthy; I am a good person; this is difficult, but the effort will be worth it in the end; my family may not understand depres-sion now, but they will when I educate them and they see how much I have changed. It made all the difference in my healing.

I've talked about how I used to compare myself to others, especially to my sisters. I never embraced who I was and what made me special because my inner dialogue was not embracing the good qualities I had to offer. We all have positives and negatives in our lives, things about ourselves we are proud of, and things we are not. Focus on the positives, and stop the comparisons. There is always someone in a better situation than we are and always someone in a worse situation. Embrace who you are, what you have, and what you have to offer.

Think about this cycle: our thoughts control our behavior and our feelings; our feelings control our behavior and thoughts; and our behavior affects our thoughts and our feelings. So, essentially, it is impossible to run and hide from yourself. Don't waste your time trying to do so. Instead, define your goals, create positive affirmations and visualizations to help you reach those goals, and listen to that positive inner dialogue. Never give up. Be intentional about what you want to achieve. And mean it!

If you simply make an "I am" statement, it is not going to work. However, if you state it with emphasis and specificity, such as "I am going to do this!" you will eventually begin to believe your own words, and your life will be rewarded with endless possibilities.

CHAPTER 28

TOOL #8 – NURTURE YOURSELF!

Do something for you

"I just want to start my life over. I want to finish my bachelor's degree and get my own place. Write a book. Get my master's. Continue to learn about myself and apply all the new teachings I've learned (at South Coast) to my life. I want to leave Southern California and go to Portland, Seattle, Denver, Idaho, Telluride, Vermont, Alaska. I don't know where, but anywhere other than here.

"I feel stuck, aggravated, irritated, unmotivated, every word in the dictionary you can think of. I want to get out of this noose. Denise bugs me. Dogs bug me. I want and need silence. I don't want to be bothered by anyone or anything. I just want to start my life over somewhere else. I feel I am so irrational with my thinking. Noise is acute. Every sound can set me off. I feel suffocated in my own skin. I feel like my world is caving in, yet my mind and body are growing and trying to get out of this tight bubble that prevents change, growth, or even just a little smile."

– November 14, 2004

I find it interesting how intertwined all of the coping tools are. In that passage above, I was journaling, which was good. I was breaking free by releasing some stress and chaos, which was good. I was expressing myself, which was good. But I was also creating stress and chaos with all of my negative com-

ments. Those negative comments were part of my inner dialogue I was listening to, but I was not reversing those negative
words into positive affirmations. See how difficult this is? And
we've still got a handful of tools to go. Coping with depression is a lot of work all the time. Utilizing one or two tools at
once may not be enough. Three or four may not be enough. It
depends on the situation you are in. But once you learn them
all and implement whichever ones you need at the right time,
the rewards will be immeasurable.

One tool I should have been applying as I was writing
that in my journal was *Nurture Yourself!* Wherever your happy
place is, go there, even if it's just in your mind. After journaling, I should have laid down, closed my eyes, and gone to
Alaska or Portland or Denver. I should have tried to think of
something positive about Denise. I should have looked at pictures of our late dog, Kato, which might have made the dog
barking outside more tolerable. I should have walked down to
the beach and enjoyed the sights and sounds. Visualize what
your life would look like if it were stress and chaos free. What
if it were noise free? You can have it, even if it is only in your
mind. Sometimes that is all we need to take those breaks and
change our attitudes.

For those who work full time every day, consider taking
a walk during your lunch time instead of working through
lunch or running errands. When you are getting ready for bed
in the evening, spend a few extra minutes taking a bath instead
of a shower. Spend time throughout your day with people
who make you happy, and avoid those who bother you. Add
a screen saver on your computer that simply says "Breathe"
to remind you to just breathe throughout the day. You will
be surprised how often we do not breathe, especially in tense
situations, and how much breathing can help calm us. Take a
five-minute break from work or chores by taking a trip to the
bathroom. Sounds like a strange thing to say, but it's one place
where you can generally be guaranteed some privacy.

As I have mentioned numerous times, my house was and
still is chaotic to no end. People are always coming and going.
The door is revolving. There is rarely silence. I have to make

an effort to find some. But it's worth it. And when I do find it, I cherish every second of it.

Some more ideas: Light scented candles around the house and enjoy the warmth and aromas they produce. Go to a movie, even if it's by yourself. If you feel like laughing, pick a comedy. If you want to release some stress but aren't in the mood to laugh, maybe an action movie with lots of explosions would be better. Take a scenic drive with your favorite music playing, or keep the music off if you prefer silence. Pick a road without a lot of traffic and pedestrians. Roll the windows down if it's nice out and enjoy the breeze. Do whatever relaxes you.

One thing I sometimes do today that I started doing years ago is keep my radio off when I'm in the car. It's natural to turn on the radio as soon as we start the car to find a song to fit our mood. But try not doing that. From a personal standpoint, it is one of the best things I do for my sanity. No voices talking or singing. Total silence. It's a perfect time to listen to yourself breathe, a perfect time to tune out life. You will be amazed at how much your stress level can be reduced.

With life at home being hectic with my dad's disease and with the many educational, personal, and professional responsibilities I had to tend to during the writing of this book, I was stretching myself too thin and neglecting my own nurturing practices. I kept up with yoga until my classes at school and appointments with clients for my practicum fell on those days.

On certain days I helped Mom with my dad, which wasn't usually scheduled since each day depended on how he was feeling. And then I'd be so tired at the end of each day that I would plop down in bed to watch TV or log on to Facebook instead of unwinding with quiet time and/or journaling. Once I realized what I was doing, or not doing, I changed my unhealthy pattern by unplugging from technology. I was then able to read, write, and relax until I fell into a peaceful sleep. There is no doubt that most of us today spend more time than we should with social media, video games, texting, and other technology. Allow yourself time for those activities, but structure your time. Set those activities aside at certain times of the day, and engage in them for shorter periods of time. You can do without them, or at least with less of them.

I once read an article in *Yoga Journal* about a vice president of an Internet search engine company. He shared how he does a forty-five-minute meditation in the morning when he first gets up. He then showers and gets ready for work. He still has not looked at his cell phone. When he gets in his car to head to work, he still does not look at his cell phone. Instead, he takes in all of the beauty and sounds around him. He begins his work day only when he reaches his office. So if the vice president of a search engine company can do it, why can't we? We can!

Notice with these tools that if you use them, good things can happen. But if you don't use them, the opposite can happen. It's not just that nothing will happen if you don't use them, but bad things could happen. In the case of the nurturing tool, doing something to bring you a sense of calmness can be very beneficial. Not doing something can leave you emotionally and mentally exhausted, causing an abundance of problems throughout the day, some that could be physically or mentally devastating.

Find what actions make you happy and do them every day. Just like you would schedule an appointment with a doctor or time to run an errand that has to be done, set aside some time each day for happiness. It will be time well spent.

CHAPTER 29

TOOL #9 – EXERCISE AND NUTRITION!

Get fit, stay fit, feel good

"I broke down in tears again. The nurse said it may be from too much stimulation at one time. Then I called Mom and she said, 'I'm here for you. Whatever it takes, Tanya. We'll make sure you're out of bed by 9 A.M. We'll have a cup of coffee, get dressed, go for a walk.'"

– October 16, 2004

Exercise does not need to be at a gym or in formal classes. You just need to get out and get moving by walking, running, doing yoga or Pilates, lifting weights, jumping rope, doing jumping jacks – whatever it takes to get you up and out and breaking a sweat. Do whatever it takes to get your blood briskly circulating throughout your body, from your head to your toes. Park a little farther away from your destination. Take the stairs instead of the elevator. I mentioned earlier that I try to take daily walks with my mom. It is a great way to exercise the body and mind as inevitably I talk to her about what I am thinking that day. And make the walks, or whatever exercises you are doing, by scheduling them. Carve out that time each day, whether it's for fifteen minutes or an hour, to make sure you are exercising in some form.

When it comes to eating, eat right. I know that's a cliché passed down for generations, but given the many health issues in today's society, such as obesity and diabetes and cardiovascular disease, many of us are obviously not paying attention to it. Drink a lot of water, oftentimes in lieu of food. I have learned that sometimes I feel hungry, but what I really am is thirsty. More water and less food may be all we need. If you feel hungry, drink a glass of water first and see how you feel.

I have learned that one of the primary keys to eating healthy is to listen to your body. Listen to that voice inside you when you are about to put something into you. If you are about to consume something – food, alcohol, or drugs – and you are feeling guilty about it, then don't do it. If you are feeling any shame about it at all, that's the voice telling you to stop. Limit your sugar intake. Do not purchase the enormous sodas. Don't supersize your meals. If you are lying around watching television and the voice is telling you to get off your butt and exercise, listen to it.

Many times I feel myself getting run down because I'm trying to cram too much into my day, so I reach for that energy drink and down it like it's a magic potion. I know that stuff isn't good for me. I know it because the voice inside is telling me so. It's telling me by causing me to become anxious and jittery. I don't need an energy drink. I need to slow down and get more rest. It's similar to a car that sputters because it doesn't have enough oil. That sputtering is your car telling you to feed it. And what happens if you feed it water instead of oil because water is cheaper or more accessible, just like we often treat our bodies with food? Eventually it will damage your car, possibly beyond repair. Listen to your body. It's smart. It knows what it needs and doesn't need. It knows what is good for you and what is not.

What is also good for you, and your body knows it, is sleep, but it's something many of us do less of as we get older because we become busier. Doctors will often say we all need six to eight hours of sleep a night. Nobody knows your body and mentality better than you. If you sleep six hours, that may not be enough. Eight might actually be too much, leaving you with a heavy head in the morning. Figure out how much you need to properly function each day and then stick to that schedule. Without quality sleep we become irritable, impaired, yawn excessively, or hallucinate. Our immune system becomes impaired, and we increase our susceptibility to diseases.

I began Chapter 18 with a journal entry about the lack of sleep I was getting since I had arrived at South Coast: *"I haven't slept regularly in five days. My body and mind are very tired."* I was very ill-tempered then, and it showed in my writings. It would be interesting to see how much more positive of a person I would have been had I simply been able to sleep. Again, listen to your body. A yawn or tired eyes are your body telling you to call it a night. Too many people feel guilty because they feel like sleep is the equivalent of doing nothing, of not being productive. But you need that sleep to effectively be productive when you are awake.

A lack of sleep can decrease our reaction time. It can cause headaches and tremors. It can even cause psychosis. For example, you have probably seen a crime show on television where investigators try to break down a suspect. They will use various techniques to do it, one being to pump the suspect up on caffeine and cigarettes, keeping him sleep-deprived until he can no longer take the pressure. He finally snaps. I know that "snap" all too clearly.

The bottom line when it comes to food and rest: listen to yourself. If you do what your body is telling you to do when it is telling you to do it, you will find your energy levels increasing and overall health improving.

CHAPTER 30

TOOL #10 – PROBLEM SOLVE!

Set your goals

"I am trying to live at the end. I am visualizing what I want to achieve. I know the power of the intention is there, and I will bring it forward every day of my life."

– March 15, 2005

One of the biggest pieces to solving the depression puzzle is having the ability to solve problems. I said earlier that using a calculator is not an option. Each problem that comes your way needs to be broken down into its parts for you to not only solve the problem, but to understand how you solved it.

During my hospitalization, I was given worksheets out the wazoo every day. They made me think, kept me busy, and forced me to stay disciplined in my problem-solving skills. One worksheet the staff at South Coast gave me was a problem-solving/goal-setting paper. I needed to identify one specific task in my journey toward mental wellness that I wanted to take on. It could be something personal, professional, financial, social, spiritual – whatever I wanted. Once I identified it, I needed to determine what standard I would use to measure my progress, along with the length of time for which I would do it.

For example, the task I chose was to create a schedule of my daily activities and to stick to that schedule as soon as I finished the outpatient program and was on my own again. The

197

standard I would use to measure my success was the amount of time I spent in isolation doing nothing (in my room or wherever) versus the time I spent doing activities. The busier my day was and the less time I spent in isolation, the more successful I was. My plan was to do this for one week.

The next step on the worksheet was to identify any possible problems or obstacles I might encounter while working toward my goal. Mine included anxiety, lack of energy, the desire to avoid interacting with people, the challenge of managing my time after having it structured for me by South Coast the past three months, and procrastination.

Next I had to identify possible ways to overcome those problems or roadblocks. My answers included buying a daily planner, scheduling chores and activities to keep me busy, meditating, exercising, reading a book or reviewing what I had learned at South Coast, and finding a new hobby.

The last step was to list what I would do to achieve my goal while prioritizing my steps. I said I would plan out my entire week, abide by that schedule, stay focused on each task, and remember the feeling of accomplishment throughout the process.

At the end of the week, I filled out a progress report to document how I did. After reiterating what the problem was that I was trying to solve, the standard I would use to measure it, and for how long I would do it, I had to identify the actual roadblocks I encountered.

"I did a good job. I didn't isolate myself. However, I did notice on the last day, when I was planning to do something with my mom, she wasn't home yet from what she was doing and I started to get anxious," I wrote.

I then had to rate myself for the week.

"I think I was very successful, but I did rely too much on my mom and her friend to do stuff with," I stated.

I concluded the progress report by writing down what I learned for the week." *I am realizing that I am having difficulty with filling my time with activities,"* I said. *"Structure is difficult for me, and I need to find a system that will work."*

I then immediately began working on identifying a problem I wanted to tackle the following week to keep myself in the flow.

The key to problem solving and goal setting is breaking it down and writing it down. I could have just said "I am going to make a schedule this week to keep busy and I'm going to stick to it." If I didn't break it down into what I was specifically going to do to keep busy, or if I just tried to keep track of it all in my head, I never would have accomplished my goal. Instead, I probably would have gone in the opposite direction because of the anxiety I would have brought upon myself.

Problem solving can be tedious, just like doing a math problem. But once you have solved it, there is no greater feeling in the world.

Chapter 31

Tool #11 – Get Real!

Live Authentically

"Why was it that it was so important for me to fit in? I always felt out of place. I was taller and bigger than others, and I wanted to be small and petite. I always thought that was one of the reasons why I never had a boyfriend in high school. I always tried to fit in by going to parties, drinking. I was so insecure."

– March 7, 2005

Getting real with yourself can be a very difficult task, but it can also be one of the most rewarding tasks because it guides you toward living an authentic life. To live authentically means to have integrity; say and do what you mean. Don't lie to yourself. If you feel that a relationship is not right, move away from it. And don't promise anything that you can't deliver, even if it is something as small as a "Let's do lunch" statement. How many of you have said that and never even attempted to make it happen? I know I have been guilty of it.

It took me many years to realize how disingenuous of a life I was leading at times. It went all the way back to high school when I was trying to be like my sisters who were so smart and beautiful. I thought if I had what everyone else had, or acted the way I thought people expected me to act, I would be a happier person. Nobody ever put pressure on me to "fit in" better at school or to be more like my sisters. I did it all to myself, in my own mind. I wasted so much time trying to live according to some fake rule book that I thought everyone else had instead of following my own true and unique self.

Take it from experience: stop comparing yourself to others, and stop looking for happiness outside of yourself. You will only end up disappointed and will send yourself spiraling into deep despair. Nothing is worse than compromising yourself to the point where you get yourself down. The only person or thing that can make you truly happy is you. Tap into whatever brings you joy. If time and money were not an issue, what would you be doing with your life? Answer that question, then try to find a way to make a living doing it. If you cannot quit your job or move to another state or do whatever it is you really want to do because of financial or family obligations, then do whatever it is you love a little bit each day.

If you love woodworking, work on projects on the weekends. If you love to write, wait until the kids go to bed, find a quiet room, and write. If playing music is your passion, find or start a band and play in your free time. Sure, you may be tired at the end of an already long day or week, but you will generally find plenty of energy when you are about to do something that involves your true passion. And with time, who knows what will happen. You may be able to turn that passion into something more than just a side gig.

When I was going through my graduate program, I had to do a practicum at the end of the academic course work. For those ten months I was not living authentically because I realized in the midst of the practicum that I no longer had the desire to be a therapist. I was there just so I could get my degree. It was a huge struggle for me to go in each day. The problem was I had come so far that I did not want to quit. It put me in an interesting quandary: do I live authentically and just quit in the middle, or do I live an inauthentic life and push through until I have that master's degree in hand? I considered the latter option to be the better choice.

Though living an inauthentic life for a while, I was being real with myself by admitting that I did not want to be a therapist when I was finished. I was not going to force myself to obtain a job as a therapist after I earned the degree just because that was my original reason for going to school. What I decided I really wanted was to be a full-time speaker and life coach. So when I wasn't in school or doing homework, I worked on my coaching business and continued scheduling speaking engagements for the weekends. It was a ton of work, and I was exhausted. But I ended up diving into coaching and speaking full time and had a master's degree to show for all of my hard work, which also gave me more credibility and expertise in my professional life.

I hear people all the time say how much they hate their jobs and that's fine. I understand you may not be able to just up and quit. But you can still do something about it in your free time. And if you don't feel like you have free time, go back to the first tool I talked about and schedule time to do what it is you love. You will also be implementing the third tool by breaking free from the stress at work, even if just temporarily each day or week.

I admire young people who come out of high school and decide they are going to backpack through a foreign land before going to college. Who says you have to go to college immediately after high school? If you want to travel abroad for a year and can afford to do so, then do it. Or the high school star athlete who also wants to be a doctor and decides medicine is really what he wants to focus on. He ignores all the outside pressure and gives up an athletic scholarship to pursue the career he really wants. It takes guts to do that. It takes authenticity.

Whatever you do, be real. Be authentic. Be you.

CHAPTER 32

TOOL #12 – ACCEPT AND SURRENDER!

What We Resist Persists

"The largest challenge for me was to accept where I am now. I finally surrendered. I became so open to so many possibilities."

– March 15, 2005

"God, grant me the serenity to accept the things I cannot change; courage to change the things I can; and wisdom to know the difference." There is the *Serenity Prayer* again, right in line with the coping tool *Accept and Surrender!* We have to trust. Lean on God, or your higher power, to get you through your depression as you rewrite your story. The past cannot be changed, so don't live in it. It is way too easy to stay there and make your situations your identity. That "it is what it is" phrase irritates the heck out of me sometimes because I think people should get ruffled over certain situations, but they don't. They choose to be happy instead. Then I think, "Wow, what a peaceful way to work through that challenge."

Refrain from thinking about what you believe should have been, would have been, or could have been. Avoid saying to yourself, "I just wish I had seen the signs." You cannot undo anything that has happened. The only thing you can change is your response to what others say and how you react to events or people.

My mom, since day one of my youth, has always said, "The way things are happening is how they are supposed to happen." My mom says this about everything. She has accepted everything that she has faced, including the death of her daughter. Accepting a situation does not mean it is your best friend; you are not inviting it in for a cup of coffee. Rather, you are saying, "There is nothing I can do about it; it is what it is and I have to move forward and away from it."

Accepting a situation "as is" does not mean you are a victim, but a victor. You are releasing that toxic energy that has consumed you. If I did not accept the fact that my sister was murdered, that my two best friends died, and that my ex-fiancé canceled our wedding, I would still be in a psych ward. My mom's attitude helps me get through those rough times. Don't allow tragedy, loss, or other painful experiences to be your identity. You need to, in a sense, embrace the bad and love it so you can be at peace with it. That does not come naturally to most people because we are often taught to be resentful and vindictive, to hold on to anger and hate. I want to be a messenger, speaking from experience, of how much more productive your life can be if you can accept your depression, disability, or loss. Once you arrive at that state, then you can surrender to it by asking, "Okay, what is next?" and focus on what you need to do to get well again.

For example, in 2006 I went to the doctor for what I expected to be a routine physical, but there turned out to be nothing routine about it. The doctor found a small mole on my leg, one that had been there for years and to which I had never given much thought. He didn't seem too concerned, but ran some tests on it anyway. Four days later, he called to say it was melanoma and I had to have surgery immediately. When the surgeon was finished with the operation, I had lost a chunk of flesh in my leg and had twenty-nine staples holding the gaping wound together. The surgeon also said he injected a dye into me during surgery that would reveal if the cancer had entered my lymph nodes, but that it would take a couple weeks to get those results back.

From the time I found out I had melanoma until the surgery, and from the time of the dye injection until I received the results (which, thank goodness, were negative), I was a nervous wreck. I struggled to sleep and eat. I worried nonstop. I had to try to implement some of the tools I'd learned less than two years earlier. It wasn't easy, and I'm not sure I would have been able to cope with the anxiety had I not had the support of my parents and sisters. They helped me to accept and surrender. I did all I could do on my own by following the doctor's orders and focused hard, with my family's help, on not worrying about what I could not control.

Another time I accepted and surrendered was that time in the church pew in 1996 when I asked God to help me forgive. It was at that moment I chose to accept the reality that my sister was not coming back and that, in my mind, her ex-husband did this to my family. I accepted and surrendered to my faith to help me move on. I did not get over it … I moved on. There is a huge difference. I don't believe anyone ever gets over such horrific events, but you can learn to move on without that person, or whatever your situation may be.

If you have an emotional breakdown, don't be the victim of your circumstance. Be a student of life as I eventually chose to be. I finally embraced the crisis in my mind. I wanted help. I wanted to accept and surrender and be managed back to good health. Only then could my treatment start. Acceptance did not and could not come until I asked for it. I needed to accept my hospitalization for me to stay safe and grow. I needed to accept the situation and surrender the pain to my God. To do that, I needed to find the strength to do it. Remember the *Serenity Prayer*.

CHAPTER 33

MEDICATION

"My doctor said he was going to give me something called Risperdal for anxiety. I took half of one and was fine. Then I took another half later and got sick. Then I took one whole one and couldn't sleep at all, and I had horrible dreams."

– December 8, 2004

I am not an expert by any means on medication, and that journal entry above was not a knock at all against Risperdal. Half a pill worked perfectly fine for me. More than that did not work for me. The key words there are "for me."

I have three hard rules I follow when it comes to medication of any kind for mental health: be your own advocate by listening to your body and telling your doctor what it is saying, take it only as prescribed, and it should not be solely relied upon to get better.

Looking back at my medical records from South Coast, on October 13, 2004, my psychiatrist put me on Lexapro for anxiety and depression. He also put me on Effexor for anxiety, depression, and panic disorder. The next day he doubled the dosage of Effexor, stating that I remained "very depressed, tearful, angry" when I met with him that day. I was also having a difficult time sleeping, so he added the sedative Ambien to the mix.

On October 15, my psychiatrist raised my Effexor again, citing anger I was feeling toward my ex, along with my anxiety about the *National Enquirer* article that was going to be published. A day or two later it was raised again to an amount that was quadruple the initial dosage I was given when I was first admitted, but that much caused me to go into an extreme anxiety state, almost manic. I was getting agitated with absolutely everybody, even fighting with the nurses. That's when we knew the Effexor dosage was too high.

On October 18 and 19, I was taken off the Ambien because it wasn't working and was put on Restoril. I was also given Xanax to help reduce some of the anxiety.

I share all of this with you to show that when it comes to medication for mental health issues, you are very much like a guinea pig in the early stages. Every person is different and, therefore, every person reacts differently to various drugs. That is why you must be your own advocate by listening to your body. If something doesn't feel right, tell your doctor. Have your dosage or drug changed, if necessary. Don't think if what you have been prescribed is not working that it will magically get better with time at that same dosage level.

To extend that to my next rule, if the dosage of medication you are taking does not feel like enough, tell your doctor and see if he agrees the amount should be raised. Do not take more than has been prescribed, assuming that a higher dose will make things better. In other words, don't abuse it. According to the National Institute on Drug Abuse, an estimated twenty percent of people in the United States have taken medicines for reasons beyond what their doctors prescribed, which has contributed to a host of other problems, including an increase in violence and suicides.

Medications can have very serious side effects which, of course, increase if you take more than what was prescribed. I am proof of what taking too much can do. I was supposed to take that Klonopin back in 2004 on an "as-needed" basis. I was taking it far more than I needed, and I was ignoring the warning label about taking it with alcohol. It nearly fried my brain to the point where I almost took my own life.

My other mistake with the Klonopin was I assumed, even if I had taken the correct amount, that it was supposed to take care of my problems on its own, which highlights my third rule about not relying solely on medication. I had no idea what coping skills were or any other techniques that could have helped me overcome my stress and anxiety. I took a pill and that was it. Isn't that what everyone did? Isn't that what the pills were for? To cure you of your problems? You cannot rely on medication alone. Use the coping tools and other methods or products that can holistically calm the brain: meditation, a hot bath, soft music, candles. Turn off your technology and let the brain relax.

Always remember that life happens every day and with that inevitably comes stress and chaos at various levels. Medication can help if you listen to your body and take it as prescribed, but you cannot rely on it alone. Taking a pill will, at best, only calm you for the moment. Couple it with the right coping skills to help you get control of your difficulties.

CHAPTER 34

NICOLE, HERISSA, AND TROY

"Pope John Paul II died on Saturday. Although I was born and raised Catholic, I never knew much about him. I never knew all the good he did in breaking down communism, in promoting world peace. He loved all people of all faiths. I have never known any one person who has truly 100 percent unconditional love for everyone. As I watch the montages of him, I see a man, a person, and a human child of Jesus, always in prayer, always in love with Christ. A man who loved children. A man who loved poetry, sports, and acting. He had interests outside of being Pope!

"I think when someone is in such a position of authority and respect, we lack the ability to humanize these figures. If I knew the Pope on a personal level, I would picture him just enjoying dinner with his family, just like a 'real' person. He has opened my eyes to the fact that I am missing my personal relationship with Christ. Thank you for that, Holy Father. Thank you for opening my heart on life and dying. You are a courageous warrior, and will be missed. I love you, and welcome home."

– April 4, 2005

It's amazing for me to read that journal entry about the Pope and believe I wrote it, that I so swiftly and peacefully came to terms with his death. No, he wasn't a family member or friend, but for me to have that positive attitude about anybody's death after all I had been through – to be able to see all of the good in him and have the mental wherewithal to eloquently say "thank you" and "welcome home" without any stress – was a solid indication of how far I'd come in the six months since I started my treatment.

I am often asked: "So how exactly did you come to terms with the deaths of Nicole, Herissa, and Troy?" And the answer is never a quick or simple one. That's because there wasn't necessarily one defining "aha!" moment. With Troy, as I will explain, maybe there was a little bit. But as much as people would like a black-and-white answer, you have learned that very little in regard to depression is black and white. It is a process and generally a very long one. It takes many moments – dozens, hundreds, thousands – small and large over the course of months or years for depression to be managed. It was the same way for me in coming to terms with their deaths.

Obviously, using the coping tools has been the key. *Accept and Surrender!* is the apparent one. But I have also identified and managed my thoughts about the three of them and given gratitude for what they each gave me in their short times here. I continually express my feelings about them in a joyous way.

Herissa taught me so much by just being herself, by being authentic. Through her death, she taught me to never lie, especially to a friend. I talked previously about how I lied to her as to why I couldn't go with her to the festival. I did it to not hurt her feelings, but I never should have felt like I had to withhold the truth from a friend. If she were such a good friend, why could I not be real with her? I could have. It was a huge mistake on my part, one that I learned from the hard way, and one I have tried to never repeat.

Herissa's funeral was at a local park overlooking the Pacific Ocean. People today often refer to a funeral as "a celebration of life." Well, Herissa's funeral literally was a celebration of her life. Everyone wore light, bright colors, a true reflection of who she was. There were balloons, music, and a lot of smiling faces as we reminisced about her. Wow! How she would have absolutely loved that send-off!

Any time I feel like I am about to fall back into depression, I think of Herissa. I think about how happy she always was, how she took life in stride, how she saw the good in everybody – even those who were not so good. She had triggers – we all do – but her blissful approach to life enabled her to squash them like little, insignificant bugs. I envision her hanging today with Troy and Nicole. They were all free spirits, adventurers, who would have loved to fly. I can see her confidently leading the way as they glide together through Heaven, laughing and having a great time.

I still tear up when I talk about Herissa today. But I smile at the same time. That's the difference between then and now. Today I remember her for what I had with her and for the positive impact she still has on my life today, not for what I lost. And that makes me happy.

Coming to terms with Troy's death happened partly because of an "aha!" moment – the day I went to his parents' house and saw them filled with the Holy Spirit. That incident showed me that if they could be happy, I could be happy. It showed me that I needed to reconnect with Christ, my higher power, through prayer. Without it, I never would have had the thought or motivation to find a church I felt comfortable with, or to get baptized. Troy used to talk to me about his newfound faith, but never pushed it on me. He taught me to seek God during the good and bad times, but left it up to me to do it. It took me a while, but I'm glad I listened. I am who I am in my relationship with God not just because of the way my parents raised me, but because of Troy. He taught me that it's not about religion, but about my personal relationship with God. I got it. I finally got it.

Troy went through so much heartbreak when his dad died. It turned him into someone he wasn't. Now that I know what depression is, I can see how he likely suffered with it. His initial response to his father's death was to drink until he was out of his mind and lash out at the world. But with support from his family and me and others who loved him, he sought help. He showed that the worst thing he could have done after his dad died was to try to hide from the grief and pain. He eventually faced it, and he became an amazing human being.

Troy left a memory of himself in people's minds that if you are going to do something, do it hard, do it big, do it right, and make it happen. He was ambitious in everything he did. Nothing he tackled was small, insignificant, or light. He did everything with the extreme intention of getting it done and having fun.

I have no doubt Troy is the party guy in Heaven, smoking a cigar and playing poker. His male friends buried him with a royal flush in his hands. Nothing could have been more appropriate. His life was one big gamble. Sometimes he won, sometimes he lost. And while I initially felt like he lost when he died, I eventually figured out during my treatment that he actually won the greatest of all victories. And not just with a full house or four of a kind, but with that unbeatable royal flush. He found hope. He found happiness. He found mercy. He found love. He found peace. What more could any of us want?

Nicole … wow! It is difficult to figure out where to begin. I remember how sad I was after she died and how hard it was to grieve because of the unusual circumstances behind her death. But after my treatment, I was amazed at all of the wonderful things about her that flooded my brain.

The woman loved life. She loved to entertain, and she went all out when you visited, whether it was for coffee, lunch, to play tennis, to have drinks, to eat dinner. You always felt special walking into her world. She was always present and listened with compassion. She loved her kids, baking cookies with them just because, decorating their lunch pails, hand-making their birthday invitations. She was very engaged in their lives every day.

Nic invited friends who had nowhere to go for the holidays to spend them with her family in celebration at Rockingham. She treated everybody with respect, the way she wanted to be treated. I remember a woman from Brentwood telling me a story of how Nicole was standing behind her in line at a floral shop and the woman was short on the money she needed to buy the arrangement she wanted, so Nicole gave her the money. Not a big deal to Nicole, but that random act of kindness impacted the woman so much that for years she left beautiful tropical flowers on Nicole's grave. Nicole had that effect on people. That presence. That warmth.

Nicole was a huge James Taylor fan. Roger Daltrey from The Who was her favorite. One day we were cruising in her car and she swore Roger Daltrey passed us going in the other direction.

"That wasn't him," I said, giving her a ridiculous look.

"No, I think it was!" she said, quite determined. And with that, she spun the car around and chased the guy down. She pulled up next to him, only to discover it wasn't him. Crazy? Yes. And I loved her for that. Spontaneous, energetic, unpredictable, yet as down to earth as anyone I've ever known.

The best thing Nicole taught me was how to be a sister. Remember those crosses we made out of palms in my church youth group that we were supposed to give to someone we loved, but to whom we hadn't said "I love you" and I gave mine to O.J.? Nicole told me once that she wished I had given mine to her instead. She said even though we were sisters, she felt like she hardly knew me. That made me realize that even though you may have known someone your entire life, family member or otherwise, it doesn't mean that you should feel you don't have to tell them you love them. Make those you love feel special, no matter how insignificant of an impact you think your words or actions will have on those people. Nicole was a pro at that.

I can see Nicole in Heaven wearing her bathing suit, shorts, flip flops, lip gloss, chewing her Trident gum, dancing, and sipping a margarita. She is talking about her kids to anyone who will listen, about how proud she is of them, and how proud she is of her family for staying so strong after her death.

"Delete the need to understand," she said to me. "We don't need to understand everything. Some things just are."

But you know what? I think I'm starting to understand more and more. I understand that she spent just thirty-five years here on earth, but she knew to make the most of every day, putting her family first. I understand that through her death, an acute awareness has been brought to the issue of domestic violence. I understand that her death has given me a platform to try to eliminate the stigma that still exists with mental illness today and to be an advocate for the millions who suffer with depression. Some things still just are. But I'm getting it. Slowly. But I am getting it.

I love you, Nicole, and I miss you. And thank you. Thank you for watching over Sydney, Justin, Mom, Dad, Denise, Dominique, the rest of our family, and me. Thank you for helping us in our efforts to follow in your footsteps and make a difference in this world. Thank you for helping us find peace amid the chaos.

Epilogue

So what does a person do after going through psychiatric care? Well, with a newfound lease on life, anything and everything she can!

I graduated *magna cum laude* in 2006 from Argosy University in Orange County, California, with a bachelor's degree in Counseling Psychology. I graduated from Argosy again in October 2013 with a master's degree in the same field. I am a certified life coach and have also been trained as a domestic violence counselor and court advocate.

Through my personal experiences and professional education, my coaching work involves me helping others develop effective skills necessary to cope with stress, anxiety, and depression. I conduct workshops and one-on-one coaching using *Tanya's Tools For Change* and the Midwest Center for Stress and Anxiety program to guide others toward mental health and prevent or manage stress and mental illness. My goal is to guide individuals to acknowledge their despair, turn their obstacles into opportunities, and find peace amid the chaos in their lives. I emphasize the significance of proper self-care in achieving and sustaining an optimal quality of life.

I also speak nationally and internationally on depression and domestic violence issues. I have had the honor of speaking at large conferences, such as The Sixth World Mental Health Conference in 2010 in Washington, D.C., and smaller venues, including several domestic violence shelters. I have also spoken at numerous colleges and universities, where depression and violence have become more prevalent in recent years.

In March 2005, I wrote in my journal:

"I want to write a book. I want to take a risk by sharing my personal story with others and hopefully move someone's spirit. I want it to be a life-saving tool that can help people make their lives enjoyable and meaningful, while also bringing peace to my own heart."

It took me quite a long time, but I finally did it. I hope you have found this book valuable and can take something from it that will bring more happiness to your life.

To book me for a speaking engagement or life coaching services, visit my web site at www.tanyabrown.net, or e-mail me at tanya@tanyabrown.net. And continue reading for some more information and resources on domestic violence and depression.

RESOURCES

Mental Health

A Mission for Michael: www.amissionformichael.com;
(949) 489-0950.

Active Minds: www.activeminds.org; (202) 332-9595.

Alcoholics Anonymous: www.aa.org; (212) 870-3400.

Alzheimer's Association: www.alz.org; 1-800-272-3900.

American Psychiatric Association (to find a psychiatrist):
www.psychiatry.org; in the U.S. and Canada, call
1-888-35-PSYCH or 1-888-357-7924; outside the U.S. and
Canada, call (703) 907-7300.

Difference Makers International: www.blueribbonstory.org;
(760) 753-0963.

Dr. Richard Granese (also a doctor at Mission Hospital),
Southern California Psychiatric Associates:
(949) 489-5564.

Family Assessment Counseling & Education Services:
www.facescal.org; (714) 993-2237.

Guiding Mindful Change: www.guidingmindfulchange.com;
(619) 297-7542.

Kim Egelsee: www.kimlifecoach.com.

Mental Health America: www.mentalhealthamerica.net;
1-800-969-6642.

Mission Hospital (formerly South Coast):
www.mission4health.com; (949) 499-1311.

National Alliance on Mental Illness: www.nami.org;
1-800-950-NAMI (6264).

National Council for Behavioral Health:
www.thenationalcouncil.org; (202) 684-7457.

National Suicide Prevention Lifeline:
www.suicidepreventionlifeline.org;
1-800-273-TALK (8255).

Sexy, Fit & Fab at Any Age: www.sexyfitfab.com.

The Bridge to Recovery: www.thebridgetorecovery.com; 1-877-866-8661; locations in Santa Barbara, California, and Bowling Green, Kentucky.

The Guidance Group: www.guidance-group.com; 1-800-908-0070.

UCSD Center for Mindfulness: health.ucsd.edu/specialties/ mindfulness; (858) 657-7000.

Women's Wisdom: www.womenswisdom.net; (760) 703-9941.

Domestic Violence

Human Options: www.humanoptions.org; 1-877-854-3594.

National Domestic Violence Hotline: www.thehotline.org; 1-800-799-SAFE (7233).

Suggested web sites for personal and professional development

Bill Philipps: www.billphilipps.com
Crime Survivors Inc.: www.crimesurvivors.com
Dan Mulhern Design: www.danmulherndesign.com
Danielle Pierre: www.theelitespeakersbureau.com
David Burns: www.feelinggood.com
Gerald Kostecka: www.powerfulh2o.com
Jack Canfield: www.thesuccessprinciples.com
James Malinchak: www.malinchak.com
Jodi Barber: www.onechoicecandestroy.com
Joel Osteen: www.joelosteen.com
John Spencer Ellis: www.johnspencerellis.com
Kelli Ellis: www.kelliellis.com
Ken D. Foster: www.asksucceed.com
Loral Langemeier: www.lorallangemeier.com
Louise Hay: www.healyourlife.com
Maggie Reese: www.runawaymind.com
Michael Hooper: www.emarketinginstructor.com
Millennium Systems: www.nextmill.net
O'Connor Mortuary: www.oconnormortuary.com

Patty Baret: www.connectionsinrecovery.com
Scott Salkin: idstm.com/author/ssalkin
The Elite Speakers Bureau: www.theelitespeakersbureau.com
Ursula Mentjes: www.salescoachnow.com
Yoga Journal: www.yogajournal.com

If a Family Member or Friend Has Psychotic Symptoms:
www.med.unc.edu/psych/research/psychoticdisorders/about/what-to-do
Meditation Information: health.ucsd.edu/specialties/mindfulness/what-is/Pages/default.aspx

Acknowledgements

Thank you to every single person, literally hundreds of you, who helped me over the years through my depression and grief. From those who offered a simple word of encouragement to those who were physically by my side for extended periods of time, I am forever grateful for your love and support.

I also want to extend my deepest admiration and heartfelt gratitude to everyone who helped make this book a reality. Your assistance and kindness during this journey have been immeasurable. I especially want to thank:

The staffs at South Coast Medical Center and Mission Hospital Laguna Beach for providing me with the tools that saved my life and that have enabled me to help others overcome adversity in their lives.

William Croyle, whose storytelling of my life could not have been portrayed by any other. Thank you for your patience with me and for believing in my story.

My family and William's family for their love, sacrifices, and contributions – Juditha Brown, Lou Brown, Denise Brown, Dominique Brown, Debra Croyle, Nick Croyle, Dominic Croyle, and Vincent Croyle.

Our agent, publisher, and those who assisted them – Ronald Goldfarb, Lois Qualben, Gerrie Sturman, and Michael Qualben.

Dennis Repenning, for your invaluable insight that gave us peace of mind with our work.

Editors Carol Daria, Judy Jakyma, Vicky Kessler, Kelli Kleisinger, Lisa Kovach, Chrissie Parente, and Sandra Rivera for your keen eyes and endless help in making this project a success.

David Le Bon, one of Nicole's childhood friends and my good friend today, for your amazing talent. I could not have asked for a better cover photo.

Those who shared their stories and endorsements for the book, and those who contributed to the book in other essential ways that have helped us spread our message of hope – Ted and Bonnie Harrison, Teri Choate Glass, Douglas Miller, Tony Dow, Kate Hughes, Debra Rosen, Tom Johnson, Casey Gwinn, Eric Hipple, Ursula Mentjes, Dr. Melanie Greenberg, Dr. John Spencer Ellis, James Malinchak, Bil Howard, Ken D. Foster, Danielle Pierre, Jeanne Rebillard, Judy Ann Foster, Carole Halley, Billie Frances, Vivian Clecak, Neil O'Connor, Patrick Reddy, Judy Twersky, Dan Mulhern, Michael Hooper, Dr. Richard Granese, Carolyn Inmon, Sonja Axelson Johnson, Kristi Hugstad, Kirk Lapple, Sean Mercer, Tanya Miller, Bill Philipps, Kim Egelsee, Susie Augustin, The Guidance Group, Rebecca Israel, Ernie Castelo, Larry Lawler, and Michael Surrey.

About the Co-author

 Co-author William Croyle is a native of Cleveland, Ohio, and graduate of St. Ignatius High School and Ashland University. He is the author of *I Choose to be Happy: A School Shooting Survivor's Triumph Over Tragedy*, and *Angel in the Rubble: The Miraculous Rescue of 9/11's Last Survivor*, which has been printed in four countries. William is a youth basketball and baseball coach, and he is a member of Mary Queen of Heaven Catholic Church. He lives in Erlanger, Kentucky with his wife, Debra, and their three sons. More information on his books is available at www.williamcroyle.com. (Photo by Patrick Reddy)

— To Order —

Finding Peace Amid the Chaos:
My Escape from Depression and Suicide
by Tanya Brown with William Croyle

If **Finding Peace Amid the Chaos** is unavailable in your local bookstore, you may order on the websites of Tanya Brown or LangMarc Publishing.

— Postal Orders —

LangMarc Publishing
P.O. Box 90488
Austin, Texas 78709-0488
www.langmarc.com
Questions? Email: langmarc@booksails.com

Or order on Tanya Brown's website
www.tanyabrown.net
or email: tanya@tanyabrown.net

Finding Peace Amid the Chaos
U.S.A. – $17.00 + $3 shipping
Texas residents add 8.25% sales tax
Canada – $20.00 + $5 shipping